Youth Matter

To: Pastor Dustin

I pray this bless your
family & you ministry

Youth Matter

Kingdom Development Kingdom Impact

Daryl Jones

Published by Point Press
PO Box 299181
Pembroke Pines, FL 33029

Cover design by Allyson Rhodes
Edited by Gabe Smith

Printed in the United States of America

ISBN 978-1-7372230-0-9
ISBN 978-1-7372230-1-6 (ebook)

Acknowledgments

I am grateful for the love and support from my family and friends who encouraged me to work on this project. I appreciate all of the youth, the parents, the volunteers, and the youth ministry staff who served with me over my eleven years in youth ministry. Serving in the role of lead pastor now, I realize how those youth ministry years were invaluable to me for my development in Christian service and pastoral ministry overall.

I thank my daughters Jazz, Joy, and Jewel who helped me sharpen my thoughts and focus for this book. I thank my ministry team in their assistance in getting this project ready for publication. Finally, I'm grateful to my lovely wife Kamica for her patience, encouragement, and support in this project. She along with our seven children, are my greatest cheerleaders, and I thank God I have the privilege of being her husband and their earthly father.

Contents

Preface

This book in some regard can be referred to as "my baby."
I served in youth ministry for eleven years as a volunteer,
part-time children's and youth pastor, to becoming a
full-time youth pastor. During that time, I encountered
youth who had questions and concerns and hungered to
know more about the faith. As I searched for materials
and resources, I found a void in Christian literature
for resources tailored specifically for youth. Now, to be
honest, the church has come a long way with producing
Bible studies and videos for pre-teens and teens. However,
we still have a ways to go in producing literature beyond
devotionals as we disciple this demographic. That is where
this book comes in.

I wrote this book out of three convictions as a Christian.
First, this book contains the lessons that I desired all of
my youth, and parents raising their youth, to know while
they were in the youth ministry I served and led for eleven
years. From the youth who served as leaders in the youth
ministry, to the youth who showed up every once in a
while, this book presents what I wanted them to know—
who God is and who they are in His mission on the earth.

Second, I wrote this book as a father to my own seven children. As a father, it is my responsibility to care for them and raise them to be productive citizens in society. But my primary job is to disciple them in the reverence and instruction of the Lord. My children engage me in many aspects of life, and this book is one resource that I want them to read for themselves as an extension of the things they hear me say when we talk in the car, at the dinner table, and around the house.

Third, I wrote this book because I wish this kind of resource had been available to me when I was a youth. I am grateful for my time growing up in Sunday school and all of the church programs I was involved in. However, I believe this type of book would have encouraged me as a youth even more to be bold in my faith, and trust and love Jesus at a higher level. Much like youth ministries today seek to create a context to minister to youth effectively, this book is written directly to youth (middle school, high school, and early college age). My prayer is that through this book, youth, and parents raising youth, better understand God's plan and purpose for these significant years of life.

Chapter 1

Introduction

I remember my first time going to the state fair, my first time at Six Flags, and my first time going to Disneyland and Disney World. Those experiences were truly amazing! If you have ever experienced any one of these amusement parks, then you know that they all have something in common. Everything about them is fun. The sights, the sounds, and the music playing around the parks are all geared towards excitement. It is all about fun. You hear the screams from people on the rides and roller coasters full of elation, mixed with a hint of fear—but always the good kind of fear that you laugh off at the end of the ride. The parks even purposely place food in certain places so that the smells excite you. Everything is to prepare you for excitement and fun.

As a matter of fact, the amusement parks fill you up with all the sugary food and drinks that you could possibly handle, so you can just go, go, go, and go until the park closes. The hope is that when it is time to leave, you will have had the time of your life. You feel like you have done it all, and you have enjoyed it all.

That is the hope of the amusement parks. Unfortunately, in today's generation, we see too many of our youth (middle school, high school, and early college age) view this time of their lives as an amusement park. Everything is supposed to be fun, and if it is not fun, then they do not care about it. It is irrelevant. That is what they think all of life is supposed to be like. Too many people miss out on the richness of life as they grow older because they have held onto the false belief that fun, amusement, and entertainment are the only things that are important. Many times, youth miss opportunities and waste time because they thought they were supposed to be seeking pleasure and fun. All of a sudden, they look up and they have missed out on preparation for the next stage of life. And even worse for others, they look up to see that they have been left behind.

This is not the only thing going on with youth, though. I found in a number of studies that a lot of youth are not even thinking about adulthood. Life is just about what's going on right now and all things concerning the present moment. This is all that seems to matter to many of them.

Times and Seasons

The honest truth is the longer you keep breathing, day after day, week after week, month after month, and year after year, you will grow older and soon become an adult. Are you ready? Are you where you were intended to be, where you were supposed to be, and where God has called you to be? That is the question on the floor. *Youth Matter* because your life belongs to King Jesus, and He desires for you to make a major kingdom impact. Embrace all that He has for you. Let's look at some principles and some aspects of your life that are worth holding dear. Think about all these days of your youth and consider what God is doing in you right now, both for the benefit of now and the future.

> **"For everything there is a season, and a time
> for every matter under heaven: a time to be
> born, and a time to die; a time to plant, and
> a time to pluck up what is planted; a time
> to kill, and a time to heal; a time to break
> down, and a time to build up; a time to weep,
> and a time to laugh; a time to mourn, and
> a time to dance; a time to cast away stones,
> and a time to gather stones together; a time
> to embrace, and a time to refrain from
> embracing; a time to seek, and a time to lose;
> a time to keep, and a time to cast away; a
> time to tear, and a time to sew; a time to keep**

silence, and a time to speak; a time to love,
and a time to hate;
a time for war, and a time for peace."
Ecclesiastes 3:1-8 (ESV)

There is something really important in these verses referencing different times and seasons. I am going to summarize it like this: there is a time to laugh and a time to cry; there is a time for fun and a time for business. The recognition of maturity comes when you know what time it is in your life. In other words, the ability to discern "what time it is" is a direct indicator of your maturity level. Is it a time to play, or is it a time to be serious? Is it a time for business, or is it a time for entertainment, excitement, and fun? As you mature, you come to understand what time it is, so that you know how to respond and act accordingly.

Our society's major problem today is this culture and mentality amongst youth in which pre-teens and teenagers see their lives as if they are only a time for the amusement park experience: have a good time with as much fun as you can! This mentality sees responsibilities, being productive, and contributing to society as the worst thing for pre-teens and teenagers to think about. The goal is to have fun and experience as much as you can until "real life"

You are the church of today, and will be leaders in the church of tomorrow

comes to get you, and then you become an adult. This worldview has become the major problem for many who are now adults, and have come to realize how important those pre-teen and teenage years were for the rest of their lives.[1]

Youth Matter

Often in church, children's and youth ministry are treated as the church of tomorrow. During my years as a children's and youth pastor, I realized that this mentality could not be further from the truth. I sought to correct this false narrative by declaring that children and youth who have placed faith in Jesus Christ as their Lord and Savior are the church of right now, today, and will be the leaders of the church of tomorrow.

This book is important for you to read right now. If you are a youth who have placed faith in Jesus Christ you are the church right now, and God has some amazing plans for your life—plans that you cannot even imagine. Since you are the church of today, and will be leaders in the church of tomorrow, it is imperative that you start to live your life for kingdom development and kingdom impact.

The intention of this book is to encourage you as a youth to understand and embrace the truth that you matter to the Kingdom of God right now. It is vitally important to define terms here for the rest of this book. The word *youth* is used here primarily to speak toward those pre-teen and teenage years of life—middle school, high school, and early college ages. While this book can be beneficial for all, this book is written directly to youth. Additionally, there is a lot of meaning packed in this word *kingdom* when we speak about the Kingdom of God. Both the Old and New Testaments are filled with messages about the Kingdom of God. The earliest preaching of Jesus is summarized in Mark's Gospel with Jesus saying,

> **"Now after John was arrested, Jesus came into Galilee, proclaiming the gospel of God, and saying, 'The time is fulfilled, and the kingdom of God is at hand, repent and believe in the gospel.'"**
> **Mark 1:14-15 (ESV)**

Jesus' first sermons announced the fulfillment of Old Testament expectations for the Kingdom of God had come in His earthly ministry. Throughout His earthly ministry, Jesus continued to teach what this all meant, which ultimately led to His death on the cross for the forgiveness of our sins, His burial, His resurrection from the dead, and His ascension back to the Father. Thus, the Gospel, the Good News of Jesus Christ, is that whosoever repents and trusts in the person and work of Jesus Christ is rescued from God's righteous judgment to live in His kingdom.

If you have repented and trusted in Jesus Christ, you have eternal forgiveness for your sins and will live in His eternal kingdom. But like those infomercials—*Wait, there's more!* You do not have to wait until when Jesus comes back to set up His eternal kingdom, because all who have placed faith in Jesus Christ are part of His kingdom right now—including you as a youth. This is why I say, *Youth Matter!*

It is important to understand what a kingdom is so that you know and understand your relationship to God and how to live out His plans and purposes for your life. A kingdom is made up of three core parts: a king, his subjects, and his domain. Let's take a look at each of these so that you can embrace what this reality looks like in your life today.[2]

A King

Firstly, every kingdom has a monarch—a king or queen. In the Kingdom of God, Jesus is the Messiah, the Christ, meaning He is the king. In all kingdoms, the king assumes responsibility. As king, Jesus is responsible to provide for, protect and build up those who are under His care—His subjects.

His Subjects

Secondly, as in all kingdoms, subjects pledge their allegiance to the king and come under the king's rule of government and provision. Thus, being part of the Kingdom of God is giving your allegiance to Jesus Christ and coming under His rule, provision, and protection.

His Domain

Lastly, all kingdoms have a domain, or territory. This domain is the land mass that the king rules over, giving provisions and protections for all in that territory. The domain in the Kingdom of God is all of creation. All that He has made is under His rule and authority.

As we see in Jesus' earliest preaching in Mark's Gospel above, as well as at the end of the book of Revelation, there is one aspect of living in the Kingdom of God at the end of the age, and another aspect of living in the Kingdom of God right now on earth as we wait for the return of Jesus Christ. This experience of living in the Kingdom of God now is experienced by the indwelling Holy Spirit who is given to all at the moment they place saving faith in Jesus.[3]

The experience of living in the Kingdom of God now, while we wait for the consummation—end of all things when Jesus returns and does away with all sin and death, setting up a new heaven and new earth[4]—is the experience of God ruling over every aspect of our lives right now as we trust and depend on Him for everything. This is why *Youth Matter* in the Kingdom of God. You do not have to wait until you are an adult to experience this kind of relationship with Jesus. God has intended for this to be your experience now.

The chapters in this book are designed to help you live as a youth designed for development and impact.

Chapter Two—Discusses how God as creator of all has made you on purpose for purpose.

Chapter Three—Helps you understand God's intention for your relationship with your parents and surrounding authorities in your life.

Chapter Four—Explains the importance of your closest friendships and relationships, and the impact they can have on your life.

Chapter Five—Discusses this stage of development you are in for the future God has for you.

Chapter Six—Challenges you to look at the impact God wants to make on the world through you as a youth.

Chapter Seven—Teaches on a practical level, the practices, habits, and disciplines you can engage in to grow in your faith.

Each of these chapters can be read in isolation, but the book is optimally intended as a logical flow, or process of development, with each chapter building on one another to produce a spiritually maturing youth on fire for Christ at the end. This stage in your life is vitally important, and God wants you to understand what He is doing.

When it comes to the life God has called and purposed you to live, there is always a season of preparation. The Lord God wants so much for your life—much more than you can imagine. And if you are going to really get a grip on what these teenage years are all about, it starts with seeing yourself as the Lord sees you—valuable!

Self-Reflection

1. What do the messages in the culture say about living as a youth?

2. What are the three most important things to you in your life right now?

3. What do you hope to gain from reading this book?

Chapter 2

Your Value

Let's take a pop quiz. Which one of these is the most valuable: gold, platinum, diamonds, or plastic? Now at first glance you read each word in order and the last one, plastic, does not seem to belong with the others in this list. Gold, platinum, and diamonds are precious metals and gems. These items are not found in abundance and are hard to come by. Due to their scarcity, the cost of them is higher than most other metals and gems on the earth. However, plastic is easy to come by, thus its price does not compare to the other four.

But I want you to think about this: how much plastic do you use and rely on daily? The cars we ride in and drive are full of plastic. The buildings we live in, go to school in, and work in are full of plastic. The smart devices we use are made of plastics. Food packaging, cleaning supplies, televisions, computers, roofs, walls, flooring, etc. all contain plastics. We rely on plastics much more than we think. So again, when it comes to how you live your life, of gold, platinum, diamonds, or plastic, which is most valuable? It all depends on how you determine value.

The first thing you need to understand and embrace when it comes to having kingdom impact as a youth is your value. In life, we know that value is typically determined by how rare something is—not easy to find or not found in abundance. We see this with things like gold, platinum, and diamonds. Value is also determined by how useful something proves to be—like plastics—and the many ways it can be used. These two adjectives determine value: rare and useful. This fact is significant because it is important for you to understand just how rare you are and how useful you are.

> **God made you and has plan for your life**

Consider your true value, what you mean to society, what you mean to the world, and what you mean to the Kingdom of God. There is no one else like you, nor has there ever been a "you" before in human history. Your genetic code, and even your fingerprints are all unique. Additionally, there are so many things you have to offer the world in your lifetime, and the world is waiting on you. This is because God made you and has plan for your life.

Anyone who has been around me long or has listened to me preach and teach has heard me ask this important question: What is the most important verse in the entire Bible? Many rattle off verses about Jesus, and His crucifixion, or His resurrection. Many quote verses about their salvation and forgiveness of sin. Others cite verses about eternal life. Even though these are excellent and extremely important verses in the Bible, they are all dependent on one particular verse. The most important verse of the whole Bible is:

"In the beginning God created the heavens and the earth."
Genesis 1:1 (CSB)

This verse makes everything else in the Bible relevant. Everything else the Bible talks about and teaches hinges on this truth. If this verse is not true, nothing else in the Bible matters. There is a God who made everything from nothing. He made the entire universe: the planets, the stars, the sun, the moon, the earth, and everything in the earth. God is Creator of all—which includes time itself. Try to wrap your mind around that truth. God is before time. We know this because this verse starts with "in the beginning." Therefore, He was before the beginning to bring the beginning into existence, namely the creation of the heavens and the earth. He has created it all! Psalm 24:1 says, "The earth and its fullness belong to the Lord, the world and those who dwell in it" (*my translation*). There is nothing or no one outside of or before God. There is nothing or no one greater than Him. He made everything and everyone, including His decision to make you, and there is only one of you.

Designer-Made

There is only one of you, and you are *designer-made*. You may have experienced this or maybe have seen on TV when someone gets a designer suit or designer dress for a dance, homecoming, prom, a wedding, or any other formal event. One can buy what's called an "off-the-rack"—a one size fits all outfit. Or, they can buy clothing that has been designer or tailor made, which gives a very different appearance. The designer or tailor picks the fabric and designs the specific look. Then they take specific measurements of the guy or girl to make sure the suit or the dress fits them perfectly.

God is the Grand Designer, and out of all of His designs in creation, He intentionally designed you. And there is only one of you. Think about that. You have a distinct fingerprint, and a distinct genetic DNA and RNA sequence. You have never existed before, and there will never be another you to come into existence. With all the options God had at His disposal, He made you the way you are. Really think about that. By knowing this truth, it is important that you do not seek to be someone else. The world does not need a replica or a copy of someone else. The world needs you. You matter. Be the *you* who God created you to be. You are designer-made; you are tailor-made. If you are reading this and feel that there are some things about you that you wish you could change, I pray that you embrace this verse:

> **"I praise you, for I am fearfully and**
> **wonderfully made.**
> **Wonderful are your works;**
> **my soul knows it very well."**
> **Psalm 139:14 (ESV)**

I love the phrase "fearfully and wonderfully made." There is heavy truth in these few words. It is recognizing that you have been made. You have been created. You did not make yourself, nor did you have anything to do with your conception. Additionally, the word "fearfully" here in Psalm 139 can also be translated to "remarkably" or "awesomely." You are remarkably, awesomely, and wonderfully made. The Creator of the heavens and the earth, who made every star in the galaxy, the One who has created all of humanity, has intentionally made you to be who you are. In God's eyes, you are awesome and wonderful! You should look at yourself in the mirror and remind yourself of this truth. Never think of yourself as being less than someone else. You are designer-made. But it does not stop there. Genesis 1:26-27 says something very significant.

> **"Then God said, 'Let us make man in our image, after our likeness. And let them have dominion over the fish of the sea and over the birds of the heavens and over the livestock and over all the earth and over every creeping thing that creeps on the earth.' So, God created man in his own image, in the image of God he created him; male and female he created them."**
>
> **Genesis 1:26-27 (ESV)**

Out of all of God's great and awesome creation, humanity is the crown of His creation. Think about this for a second. I mean really think about it! God created the heavens and the earth, the universe, and the cosmos all out of nothing by speaking them into existence and "it was so." And yet, the only thing that was created "in His image" was humanity, man and woman. Nothing else in all of creation was created in the image and likeness of God. This means that we have been given intelligence, emotions, reason, and the ability to exercise these attributes to represent God on the earth. The very crown of His creation was mankind and only mankind was given the charge of ruling over creation. This is why as you observe all other animals, great and small, smart and not-so-smart, they are all under our rule and authority. As impressive as some of these animals are, they do not measure up to humanity on the earth.

I was in a conversation with someone on this topic, and the person stated that certain animals were just as intelligent as humans, and some even more intelligent. I then asked the person about what other species or other kinds of animals on the planet could navigate life on and in the water, navigate life on the land, and navigate life in the sky like mankind does by making tools, ships, submarines, cars, and airplanes? What other animals have the ability to make a smartphone, let alone the internet? Nothing in the universe tops humanity's intelligence so that we may exercise the dominion and authority God has granted us in and over the world. We rule the world, and God has called us to be good managers of what He has given us. We are to take care of it by not wasting or abusing our environment that He has given to us.

God created male and female in His image and in His likeness. You have been tailor-made as a young man. You have been tailor-made as a young lady. God has a plan and purpose for you. Do not let the world distract you. Do not let the world distort God's creative design of how He, in His divine wisdom, made you a young man or a young woman. Do not let the world intimidate you. Do not let the world confuse you in understanding how God has formed you and made you who you are.

One of the greatest myths mankind has embraced is the myth of Darwinian Evolutionary Theory, aka Darwinism.[1] In a nutshell, this theory argues that humanity has no creator or designer, but rather is actually an accident of nature that has gone through a process of macro-evolutionary progression guided by a principle of survival of the fittest. This theory has led to a way of thinking that you, as a human, are nothing but a purposeless existence that sprang forth spontaneously leading toward nowhere. This is not only scientifically untenable when applying the scientific method, but it is false. The truth is that God has given you His unchanging word that He indeed loves you and has created you on purpose and to share in His love. You did not come from an accident of nature. You did not come from some random chance over time. You are fearfully, awesomely, and wonderfully made, and God has a designed plan for your life.[2]

Designer-Planned

God's plan for you goes hand and hand with how He has designed you. If you have ever received a toy set that needed to be put together or built, along with the pieces comes instructions and the plans to build the set. As a father, I have built doll houses, mini-kitchens, bicycles, basketball goals, and all other sorts of things for my children. Watching my sons build a whole movie scene out of Lego sets was really cool. However, the only way they were going to be successful was to follow the plans that came with the set to completion. The plans were drawn up and matched perfectly with how the pieces in the set had been made. The same is true for you and God's plan for you.

Take the book of Jeremiah. He was called by God to be a prophet in an unideal situation. God sent him to declare God's judgment against the nation of Israel due to their disobedience. We do not know exactly how old he was when he was called to be God's prophet, but he was a younger person. And it is interesting what God said to him in his call. God told him,

> **"I chose you before I formed you in the**
> **womb. I set you apart before you were born. I**
> **appointed you a prophet to the nations."**
> **Jeremiah 1:5 (CSB)**

Now, not all of us are called to be prophets of God. But I want you to take special note of Jeremiah's call to be God's prophet. Not only was it before Jeremiah was even born, but God also had a plan for his life before Jeremiah was even conceived by his father and mother. Here is something we learn in this one verse: God prepares and plans for what He has created, and what He brings forth into the world. God says, "I formed you in the womb." This means God directed Jeremiah's development in his mother's womb leading to his birth—every cell, every chromosome, and every organ. And God said, "I set you apart." Being set apart here means that God had a specific plan for Jeremiah to live out that was tailor-made for him and no one else. Jeremiah was designed by God to live out God's plan for his life.

Think about the God who made you. Ask Him what plan He has for your life. Ask the Lord,

"Why have You made me?"

"Who have You created me to be?"

"What have You created me to do?"

These are the questions that God wants you to ask Him. Do not look to the world or the culture to give you your life's plan, but look to God. When you have questions, ask your Creator. Do not look to the world to find these answers when you are looking for God's plan for your life.

Designer-Purposed

Every plan has a purpose. As we discussed above, when we follow the plans and instructions for building the toy set, it is all for a purpose to play and enjoy the toy set in a certain way. When we embrace God's plan for our lives, we then begin to live out God's purposes for our lives. We all look for purpose. We all are in search for significance. Your significance, your plan and purpose are found in your Creator. They are found in the Lord. This matters, and it is truly important to grasp this, because we live in different times and different seasons as we age into adulthood.

There is an unfortunate view of God that has crept its way into the church. This view sees God as creator, but He is really not involved in our everyday lives. This view suggests that the most important thing He desires is for us to seek to be good people and be happy in our lives. This is known as Moralistic Therapeutic Deism,[3] and this mindset could not be further from the truth. God is Creator of all and greater than all, and He is actively involved in the lives of His creation. He cares deeply for His creation and passionately wants to be in close relationship with us.

There are a number of Scriptures that talk about purpose in the Bible, but one of my favorites is found in Act 13. It says,

"For David, after serving God's purpose in his own generation, fell asleep, was buried with his fathers, and decayed."
Acts 13:36 (CSB)

This verse can easily be just passed over when reading Acts 13. This verse is found in the context of the Apostle Paul preaching in a synagogue to Jews, teaching and arguing for the truth, that Jesus is indeed the promised Messiah of the Old Testament Scriptures. While presenting his evidence of who Jesus is, he gives a history lesson, and he makes this statement about King David. The reason why he says this is to let them know that David died, was buried, and his body decayed in the ground. Paul argued that Jesus was greater than David because unlike David, Jesus Christ, the promised Messiah, who they were waiting on, would not undergo decay.[4] He was arguing for the resurrection of Jesus Christ.

However, even though Paul was teaching about Jesus here, Acts 13:36 is so cool because he spoke about David serving the purpose of God in his time, in his generation. Think about that for a second. Have you ever asked yourself what is your purpose? Let's go a little deeper. Have you ever wondered what your purpose is in your generation, the era you live in? David was a faithful shepherd over his father's flock of sheep even before he was a teenager. As a youth he was anointed king of Israel. Before he took his throne as king, as a young teenager, he served King Saul and courageously defeated the giant, Goliath, giving his nation victory over the enemy. Even though he was not a

> **You cannot even imagine how valuable to God you truly are**

perfect man, David faithfully ruled as the anointed king of Israel as an adult, brought back the ark of the covenant that was lost, and established the capital of Israel in Jerusalem. Even with all that David achieved in his life to glorify God, what he wanted most was to build the temple for God in Jerusalem. However, God told him no, but instead that job would be for his son to build.

Do you know why this is important to know? Acts 13:36 highlights that David served God's purpose—not David's self-determined purpose. God's purpose for David's life was that God be glorified through David being king of Israel so that the nation of Israel would point the world to worship the Lord as the one true God. God's purpose is to receive worship and glory that only He is due. It is great to have wants and desires in life, but you must make sure they line up with God's plan and purpose for your life.

Here's a little secret, you do not have to wait until you are an adult to start walking in your purpose. Romans 8:28 says, "We know that all things work together for the good of those who love God, who are called according to his purpose." This includes you as a youth who have placed your trust in Jesus Christ as Lord and Savior. God's purpose is that the world may know Him and worship Him as God. As a youth who trusts Christ Jesus, you are being molded and shaped into looking more and more like Jesus Christ every day, so that you may live out God's purpose for your life.

You cannot even imagine how valuable to God you truly are. Society can sometimes downplay the value youth have. It can seem like that since adults are the ones who exercise all this dominion and authority spoken of in Genesis 1:26, that youth are irrelevant until they themselves become adults, thus, making adulthood more valuable than youth. This could not be further from the truth. Look at what Jesus taught the disciples about how He views younger people, in particular, children. In Matthew 19, children were being brought to Jesus for Him to pray over, but Jesus' disciples were blocking them from getting to Jesus. Studies show that there was a cultural understanding that children were not held in high esteem in society, and thus were not to be made a big deal about. But Jesus pushed back against the culture and did not turn children away. This kind of thinking still exists today in many cases. Oftentimes, children and teenagers are not valued as much to society, other than how society can make money off of them.

Jesus had to deal with this attitude, even with His disciples that had been walking with Him for some time. In Matthew 19:14 Jesus said, "Leave the little children alone, and don't try to keep them from coming to me, because the kingdom of heaven belongs to such as these." Jesus does not want you to come to Him as an adult after you have "experienced life to the fullest" or "gotten everything out of your system." He wants the closest of relationships with you right now, as a pre-teen, a teenager, and even as a child! Jesus wants you right now, right where you are. You do not have to wait until you are an adult to commit your life to Jesus and start living out the plan and purpose He has for your life.

Conclusion

We have already learned that you have extreme value in God's eyes. Therefore, your worth and value is not determined by what the world has to say. Do not let the world distort or confuse you to make you think of yourself in ways that are opposite of what the Lord says. You are rare and useful to God in unimaginable ways that the world needs and is waiting on. Nobody else can do it. Do not be mistaken or confused about this, because God's purposes will come to pass. The very God who made the universe—I am talking about the entire universe—He made you on purpose for purpose. It is important that you realize and embrace that you, even as a youth, are part of what He is doing in the world.

Self-Reflection

1. Why is it important to know God as creator of all?

2. Why do some youth seek to find their value from others instead of from God?

3. How do you feel knowing that God made you on purpose for purpose?

Chapter 3

Your Position

God says you are valuable, and He has a plan and purpose for your life. You must embrace this truth in order to understand your position in life as a youth. I remember having a high school science project, where we had to take different kinds of little beans home and grow them. We had to look up which kinds of beans they were and what each one needed in order to grow properly. We were given a certain number of days to grow plants out of the beans and each day we had to record our measurements and findings. Through that project, I found something to be so true: you can water them, you can put feed in their soil, and you can take all of these nourishing actions, but what is vitally important is where you position them so that they can get the proper sunlight. If they were not positioned strategically to receive sunlight during the planting process, you wasted your time and energy. Position matters!

This is also true in your life. If you are not positioned properly, just like those plants sprouting from the beans, death and destruction can occur. However, if you are positioned properly, then there can be thriving, flourishing and growth. See, your position right now as a pre-teen or teenager in society and in relationships is very important for your development, and the formulation of who and what you are going to be. *Youth Matter,* and your position is crucial for your kingdom development and kingdom impact.

As a youth, you are in a position of being under various authorities in your life. These authorities take the form of your parents, older relatives, teachers, principals, law enforcement, and the government. Your position under these authorities is not a bad thing at all! The rebellion against authority in the culture today is unfortunate. I do admit that there have been too many people who have misused and have abused their positions of authority. However, do not let the failings or abuse of some take you off track from the life Christ has called you to live. The Lord, Himself, is the author of all authority. He has set order in every sphere of His creation, including human relationships. See what Colossians says about Jesus:

"He is the image of the invisible God, the
firstborn of all creation. For by him all things
were created, in heaven and on earth, visible
and invisible, whether thrones or dominions
or rulers or authorities—all things were
created through him and for him. And he is
before all things, and in him all things hold
together."

Colossians 1:15-17 (ESV)

This passage says that Jesus is over every authority and all of them serve under Him. In fact, the very concept of authority was created by Jesus and is designed to serve His purposes. Thus, it is vitally important for you to understand and embrace your position as a youth as you serve the purposes of Christ Jesus. And it starts with understanding your position with your parents.

Parents

Your relationship to your parents is much more important than you may imagine. God uses parental language all throughout the Bible to communicate His loving relationship with us.[1] Additionally, it is interesting that in the ten commandments in Exodus 20, the commandment on which all of the other commands of how we relate to the Lord and how we relate to one another hinges on is the command of how we relate to our fathers and our mothers. It is also the only command that provides the promise of a long, good life.

> **"Honor your father and your mother so that you may have a long life in the land that the LORD your God is giving you."**
>
> **Exodus 20:12 (CSB)**

God's heart for this command helps us understand our relationship to Him when we properly align under the primary authority that He has placed in our lives—our fathers and our mothers. This very command is repeated numerous times in the Bible, even in the New Testament.[2]

> **"Children, obey your parents in the Lord, because this is right. Honor your father and mother, which is the first commandment with a promise, so that it may go well with you and that you may have a long life in the land."**
>
> **Ephesians 6:1-3 (CSB)**

> **"Children, obey your parents in everything, for this pleases the Lord."**
>
> **Colossians 3:20 (CSB)**

Please take note of the promise given in this commandment: Honor your mother and your father, and *you will have a long life and it will be well with you.* This promise was not just for those in the Old Testament, but this same promise is given in the New Testament. Now, that is an incentive. God is ordering your steps, but He wants you to understand that we are called to obey, respect, and honor our parents, for this is pleasing to the Lord. Whatever age you are as a youth, this is what you need to be doing. This is your command from your Creator.

Your parents are given a job by the Lord Himself. While there are many things we can choose in life, we cannot choose our parents. Truth be told, there are good parents and bad parents. Although parents are given this job, not all do so and not all do so well. In this fallen world, there are parents who neglect or mistreat their children, while others actually take their responsibility as a parent seriously. However, this does not change how you relate to your parents.

God designed parents to have authority in your home, and their parental charge is to train you in the Lord. Going back to the Old Covenant, Deuteronomy 6:4-9 (The Shema), parents are commanded to train their children when they wake up, when they go to bed, when they are eating, when they are sitting, when they are walking down the path, and in every moment of life. Every part of life is to be instructional. Now, this does not mean you are supposed to be having Bible study all the time, but there is to be constant instruction on what it looks like to follow the Lord in every sphere of life. Ephesians 5:3 echoes this same teaching of what it should look like to follow Christ in the New Covenant. The command is for parents to be the chief discipler in the home and raise their children in the reverence and instruction of the Lord.

Now let me say this, if you are in a situation in which your parents are disobedient to the Word of God, you should seek to be the kind of youth God has called you to be in your home, and all the while pray deeply for your parents to commit to live their lives for Jesus Christ. You can be a great example in your home as your parents see your faith in Jesus on display.[3]

In my ministry experience, I have noticed that many people who have a distorted view of how they relate to God as their father also have a distorted view of their relationship between themselves and their earthly parents. It may feel like your parents are being a burden by making you go to church, or trying to get you to read the Bible, or trying to make you watch those seemingly low-budget Christian movies. Even though as a youth it may feel inconvenient, it is important and purposeful. Remember, you are called to respect, honor, and obey your parents even when it is inconvenient. There should be no slamming doors, talking back, walking out on them while they are talking, no rolling your eyes, or stealing from them. Your relationship with your parents should not be you going about only what you want to do, but rather it should be you honoring and obeying them when they give you instruction.

Honor and obey your parents to the best of your ability, regardless of how you feel about the situation. By doing this, one of the major things you learn is humility. You are learning that the world does not revolve around you. You are not the one and only consideration in the world. You matter tremendously, but you are not number one. The Lord is number one, and if you cannot respond to parental authority properly, you will never properly respond to the godly authority of the Creator of the heavens and the earth. You will not even respond correctly to other earthly authority, and that will take you down a bad path because all authorities have been created by God.

Authorities in Society

Your respect for God given authority extends to your schoolteachers, your administration, or anyone else in authority. There is this thought process and view that all authority is bad. This is not true. There are indeed evil people in the world, and there are bad leaders, so discernment is important. But authority is necessary. If you believe that *all* authority is bad, then you will go against, and even fight against godly authority, which would ultimately amount to fighting against the Lord Himself.

As we saw above in Colossians 1:15-20, all authority and the concept of authority was made by and through Christ Jesus. Even government and the concept of government is from God Himself. Romans 13:1-7 and 1 Peter 2:13-17 are clear Scriptures that governing authorities are servants of God and that all followers of Christ are to respect, participate, and obey these authorities. Now it is clear also that God's design for these authorities is to promote "good" and punish "evil." This is not always the case and committed followers of Christ are not obligated to sin against the Lord because the government mandates sin. That is where we Christians take our stand for Christ. However, it is important that we view earthly governing bodies as God's design, even in a fallen world. Every government whether it be kings, queens, emperors, prime ministers, presidents, or any other kind of authority, are set by God. There is an ordering. Again, I am not talking about bad leadership. This is about the concept of leadership and the concept of authority in the world today.

You must understand your position as a youth. There is an important historical account of four youth who were taken into a foreign land against their will. In the book of

Daniel, King Nebuchadnezzar of Babylon and his army ransacked the southern kingdom of Israel. They had deported the people of the region back to Babylon. King Nebuchadnezzar chose leaders from among the young generation of Jews and developed a three-fold strategic plan to reshape a generation of Jews: isolation, indoctrination, and identification. Among them were four Hebrew youth from the nation of Israel that would go through three years of training and then serve the king. The goal was to instruct and inundate them into the culture of Babylon in efforts to make them lose their identities as Israelites, the covenant people of God, and make them Babylonians. This was a strategic plan to indoctrinate the youth so that the next generation of people would forget about the Lord, serve their Babylonian gods, and become "one of them."

Step 1: Isolation
King Nebuchadnezzar brought in the four Hebrew youth, who were the best and brightest amongst their peers; Daniel, Hananiah, Mishael, and Azariah. His isolation plan consisted of separating the Hebrew youth from their Jewish connections and community. This was significant. By doing this the Hebrew youth were no longer connected to the people of God, thus those close community ties, identity, and experiences became weakened and replaced by Babylonian community.

Step 2: Indoctrination

They were to be instructed, or educated, in the language and literature of the Chaldeans. This kind of instruction went beyond mere Babylonian history, but rather included their philosophy, idolatrous practices, and religious literature. This was to reshape their Biblical worldview of the Lord into a pagan worldview that leaves the Lord out.

Everyone has a worldview by which they see, understand, and interpret the world around them. Your worldview is your certain way of thinking about life and truth that becomes a kind of default thinking. For example, your computer or smartphone has a default screen. Whatever you set up as your default is where your computer or smart device automatically goes even without a command. Like this, without you even actively thinking or reasoning about things in life, your worldview is your default thinking in how you see and understand the world around you. This is important because your behavior and how you live your life directly follow your worldview.

Step 3: Identification

The Babylonian king had them renamed from their godly, Hebrew names—Daniel, Hananiah, Mishael, and Azariah. Consequently, they were given pagan, Babylonian names—Belteshazzar, Shadrach, Meshach, and Abednego. Their Hebrew parents had named them after the Lord, but the new names were names under the pagan Babylonian gods.[4] No longer did King Nebuchadnezzar want these Jewish youth identifying themselves with the Lord, creator of the heavens and the earth, but rather to identify themselves with the pagan gods of the culture in which they had been captured and residing. He no longer wanted them to place their trust, commitment, or allegiance to the Lord, but rather to become like them, worshiping and serving the Babylonian gods.

You may be wondering why I have given you this lesson in Bible history. These four youth's experiences are vitally important to understanding how you as a youth today can live in a culture around you that is consistently trying to remove you from your community of faith, constantly pushing against you following Jesus, and consistently trying to get you to identify with the world and the culture rather than the Lord. I want you to learn a lesson from these four youth. They made a stand for the Lord under challenging circumstances, and at the same time, gave respect to ungodly, wicked leadership.

During their training, these four youth were commanded by their authorities to sin against the Lord by eating and drinking the king's food which went against God's law.[5] One of the most amazing things in this passage in Daniel 1:8-16 is that the four Hebrew youth had already made their minds up that they would not sin against the Lord and that they were going to keep the Lord's command. They would not defile themselves with idolatry and unclean food. So, Daniel respectfully went to their leadership and asked for permission to not eat and drink that food.

It is here that we see God step in. After Daniel respectfully asked for permission from his authorities, Daniel 1:9 says,

> **God will step in for you as a youth. Trust Him!**

"God had granted Daniel kindness and compassion from the chief eunuch." God moved in the heart of wicked leadership, and they were given permission to avoid eating the defiling and unclean food from the king. Also, notice that Daniel presented a plan and solution to their problem, by which they were shown to be better than all their other peers. God gave them favor by making them stronger and more fit than all the other youth that were defiling themselves. They made the harder decision, taking a stand as youth for the Lord, even under bad leadership. They made the choice to both serve the Lord and respect their leadership, and God intervened. This indicates that God will step in for you as a youth. Trust Him!

In the face of all these challenges we learn a valuable lesson from Daniel and the other three Hebrew youth. Daniel did not just rebel against the king in his newfound situation, but perfectly sought out a way he could honor his ultimate authority, the Lord, and respect his newfound authority in King Nebuchadnezzar. He sought out a way to prove that his God was greater by seeking permission to follow the Word of the Lord and not participate in the king's idolatry by eating unclean food. God responded by giving them supernatural intelligence and wisdom that superseded all others that followed the king's program, thus showing that the Lord is greater.

Let's look at another example. When King David was a youth, he was under the bad leadership of King Saul. One of David's jobs was to play the harp for the king. But when he played, King Saul would try to kill him by throwing spears at him. David would simply dodge the spears and keep playing. If that were me, I would have been running up out of there. I would have been out, but David did not move until God made it known that it was time for him to make a move.[6] This is not a call to place yourself in harm's way. However, I am encouraging you to submit yourself to the will of the Lord, and let Him direct you in your actions and responses to evil and bad leadership.

On the opposite side of bad leadership, there is such a thing as good leadership. Whatever the task, good leaders give the guidance, direction, and support needed for those serving under them to get the job done. Good leaders are somewhat easier to follow than bad leaders. However, do not think that every good leader is sent by God and that every bad leader is sent by the devil. The Bible is very clear that no one rises to seats of authority outside of God's purposes. God sets people in power, and He guides the hearts of kings.[7] You must remind yourself that whoever God has in authority, God has called you to respond as God intends.

Conclusion

As you follow Jesus Christ as a youth, you may find yourself like the four Hebrew youth in the University of Babylon. Satan and demonic forces want to isolate you and separate you from the people of God. Thus, they present every opportunity for you to not go to church, Bible study, church fellowships, or Christian gatherings. The enemy wants to indoctrinate you with all kinds of alternative and false teachings that are opposed to Jesus Christ. And the world seeks to force you to identify yourself with the world, rather than who you are in Christ Jesus. The enemy does all of this so that you lose yourself and fail to live out the purpose God has for your life.

This is your reality. But this is also the exact situation God is calling you into. He wants you to make up your mind right now, and take your stand to live for Him. Now, it is necessary to have your mind already made up that you will not compromise your faith in Christ or your walk with the Lord. At the same time, you can honor and respect your authorities, even when under bad leadership.

As you live for Christ by obeying His Word, you will experience God's power in your life in ways you never imagined. You will be a witness for Jesus as all your peers and authorities see how you operate. This is huge! If you keep reading the book of Daniel, King Nebuchadnezzar comes to acknowledge that the Lord is the one, true God.[8] The king started out trying to change Daniel and the Hebrew youth, but rather, the king's life was forever changed in coming to know the Lord. God used Daniel, a youth, to change a king!

God loves to use His people, even youth, in mighty ways that even ungodly leaders can come to know the true God because of your witness. So, when you interact with any authority, honor and respect them, because they have been given authority by the Lord Himself. If they do wrong, the Lord will deal with them in His way and in His timing. It is not your job to get them right. Be the witness for Christ Jesus that He has called you to be in this season of your life. The Lord will handle the rest.

When it comes to these authorities, embrace your position, learn, and grow, because all it is doing is strengthening your walk and your relationship with the

Lord. Trust the Lord in it. Your position is crucial, and it serves a major role in your kingdom development and kingdom impact.

Self-Reflection

1. How have you been disrespectful to your parents or guardians, teachers, school administrators, coaches, and other authorities?

2. In what ways have you trusted God and shown respect to authorities in your life?

3. What can you start doing from now on to show respect and honor to these authorities in your life?

Chapter 4

Your Crowd

As you embrace your current positioning in life as a youth, it is equally important for you to be aware of your closest relationships. You may have heard the old saying, "Birds of a feather, flock together." This old saying highlights the fact that when we see birds flocking, or flying in formation, they are surrounded by the same type of birds. We see this with other animals as well—wolves, lions, hyenas, etc. Just as we see this in the animal kingdom, we also see this in human relationships. Now, I am not just talking about race, color, or even ethnicity, but the *kind* of people too. Namely, you may see a group of people of different races, colors, ethnicities and nationalities hanging out together because of certain things they have in common and views that they share. People tend to hang out with and do life with people who are more like them.

Your crowd is a great reflection of who you are as a person and how you live your life.

Understanding this truth is vitally important to your maturation and you fulfilling God's call on your life. As we have discussed in the previous chapter, the four Hebrew youth—Daniel, Hananiah, Mishael, and Azariah—are a great example of how much your crowd matters to your life. They stood with each other and encouraged one another to trust in and live for the Lord, even when their lives were on the line. The people you surround yourself with matter. Your relationships and your closest friendships can either destroy your life and your future, or those relationships can build you up and set you on the right path. It is so crucial who you allow in your circle.

Friendships

The book of Proverbs is one of my favorite books of the Bible. Proverbs is called *wisdom literature* because it is filled with principles for how we should live godly lives according to the Word of God. For example, lets read some words from the wisest king who walked the earth, King Solomon.

"Listen, my son, to your father's instruction,
and don't reject your mother's teaching,
for they will be a garland of favor on your head
and pendants around your neck.
My son, if sinners entice you,
don't be persuaded.
If they say—'Come with us!
Let's set an ambush and kill someone.
Let's attack some innocent person just for fun!
Let's swallow them alive, like Sheol,
whole, like those who go down to the Pit.
We'll find all kinds of valuable property
and fill our houses with plunder.
Throw in your lot with us,
and we'll all share the loot'—
my son, don't travel that road with them
or set foot on their path,
because their feet run toward evil and they
hurry to shed blood.
It is useless to spread a net
where any bird can see it,
but they set an ambush to kill themselves;
they attack their own lives.
Such are the paths of all who make profit
dishonestly;
it takes the lives of those who receive it."

Proverbs 1:8-19 (CSB)

When you read this, what came to your mind? It sounds like he's talking about a gang, right? You may be thinking, *they had gangs back then*? Yes, they did. Every civilization dealt with the issue of wayward youth causing different kinds of problems in society. King Solomon wrote in a generic way as a father writing to his son and telling him to be very careful who he hangs out with, who he rolls with, and who he kicks it with.

Pay close attention to the influence that your crowd has in your life. Recognize the pressure that your crowd places on you. Pressure to take advantage of others. Pressure to rebel against authority. Pressure to be angry and violent. Pressure to be apathetic. Pressure to lie, cheat, or steal. Pressure to be sexually active. If there are people in your life placing this kind of pressure on you, then you should leave them immediately. Do not let them in your circle. Avoid this crowd!

Peer pressure is a very real thing, and you must be careful who you listen to. The wrong crowd can take you down a very dark path that you may have had no intention of going down. The right crowd can encourage you to reach heights you never imagined. This is why the Bible puts much emphasis on the priority of our crowd—our closest relationships.

We read from the book of Proverbs, but let's see how the book of Psalms begins.

"Blessed is the man who walks not in the counsel of the wicked, nor stands in the way of sinners, nor sits in the seat of scoffers;"
Psalm 1:1 (ESV)

This verse is all about who you let speak into your life. It says that the truly blessed person does not give his or her ear to sinful counsel. In other words, they do not give their attention to ungodly advice. You should reject any advice that goes against the Word of God. As a matter of fact, this one verse uses what is called *Hebrew parallelism* to say the same thing in three different ways. Each way highlights a different aspect of the same truth.

This verse contrasts the blessed person with the wicked, sinner, or scoffer. In this verse, to "walk" is another way of saying to live. Thus, the first call is not to live your life by following the words of people who tell you to go against God's Word. To "stand in the way" refers to the various paths your life will go. Thus, the second call is to reject any lifestyle and direction of life that goes against God's Word. The final contrast says to "sit in the seat of a scoffer," which is another way of saying to rest on, or settle your position on. A scoffer is one who laughs at, makes fun of, or makes crude jokes about the things of God and living a godly life. Thus, the third call is to reject any mindset that does not take God's Word seriously. Additionally, the words "walk," "stand," and "sit" communicate a progression of growing more and more comfortable in sinful lifestyles. So, do not listen to any advice, or give your attention to ways of thinking that are opposed to the Word of God. Do not open yourselves up to that way of living.

Human behavior, within relationships with other people, functions much like the part of an iceberg we see above the water. Did you know that only 10% of an iceberg is visible above the water? The other 90% that we do not see remains below the surface. Like an iceberg, when we observe human behavior, there is much more going on deeper than we can actually see. Typically, human behavior stems from the values that a person holds. We act on the things that we believe to be important or valuable. For example, if I value having clean teeth and fresh smelling breath, then I will brush my teeth regularly.

Also, our beliefs shape our values. Whatever we believe to be right and true, shapes the things we value in life. For example, if I believe it is wrong to steal, then I will not shoplift and take things that do not belong to me from other people. But here is the all-important question, what typically shapes our beliefs? The answer: our relationships.

The Bible makes a statement that is imperative for you to embrace:

"Do not be deceived: 'Bad company corrupts good morals.'"

1 Corinthians 15:33 (CSB)

To be deceived is not a matter of one's opinion or one's preference. You are deceived when you believe something to be true, when in reality, it is actually a lie. For example, I remember getting to school early one morning during my senior year of high school. I was student council president that year. Someone told me that there were breakfast biscuits in the upstairs library, and we needed to get them before the first bell rang. I dashed up those steps, mouth salivating, ready to dig in. But I scurried into a dark, empty library, totally confused. Where were the breakfast biscuits? Then it hit me. I realized it was April 1st. That's right, April Fool's Day, and guess what, I was the fool at that moment. I had been deceived. I totally believed there were breakfast biscuits in the library, and I believed something to be true, that was in reality, a lie.

So, this verse tells you to not be deceived—to not believe the lie. But what is the lie? This is the lie: the crowd you hang with does not affect your walk and commitment with Christ. See, this verse gives a very strong warning that without fail, if you surround yourself with bad company, if your crowd is full of people who have no interest in living for the Lord, they will corrupt and destroy your walk with Christ, with no exception. Do not be fooled into thinking you will make things better, or that you will rub off on them.

Do not be deceived, because bad company truly corrupts good morals. The quickest way for you to get off track is to make your crowd and closest relationships with those who do not love God and do not care anything about living for the Lord. He said, do not be deceived and think it is going to be cool to roll with them, and think you will remain walking

> **Surround yourself with people that are going to build you up and encourage you**

consistently with the Lord. No! Do not be deceived. You will find yourself drifting down the wrong path. Do not fall for it.

Make your closest relationships and friendships with people who are trying to walk this life out to the glory of Christ Jesus. I am not talking about perfect people, because they do not exist anyways. However, you can surround yourself with people that are going to build you up and encourage you. Make your crowd people who are going to point you to the Lord, and point you in the right direction. Make your closest friendships with people who will hold you accountable when you are doing wrong, and do it lovingly to lift you up, not to tear you down. Your crowd matters to your growth in Christ Jesus.

Romantic Relationships

In the human experience, especially due to human growth and development, there are other kinds of relationships that are important to discuss when it comes to your kingdom development and impact. As you mature from adolescence to adulthood, there are certain hormones that start to kick in. You may begin to have certain physical longings, urges, and desires. Accordingly, you may begin to think about romantic relationships.

There is nothing inherently wrong with this process of development, and this is all part of God's design for all of humanity. However, it is vitally important that you understand what is occurring in your mind and body, so that you may line everything up under the lordship of Jesus Christ. God, in all His wisdom and power, designed every aspect of your body, and He has given you the freedom to enjoy all He has designed. However, He also gave boundaries to protect you as you enjoy all that He intended. This is why the Bible gives so much instruction against sexual immorality. God gives instruction so that you may fully enjoy what He is providing, even when it comes to physical intimacy.

Too often in the church setting, we have thought about sex in such a negative way. Sex gets talked about so badly that even when godly people become adults and get married, they struggle to enjoy one another intimately. Their perspective on intimacy and sex has become distorted. This is truly unfortunate because God blessed the marriage union when He created humanity. In other words, God created and blessed sexual intimacy within marriage.

As we discussed in chapter 1, the Almighty, All-Knowing God created male and female in His image and likeness as complementary beings to function on the earth as the crown of His creation.[1] He blessed them, and He told them to be fruitful and multiply.[2] This goes to show that physical intimacy between a husband and a wife is blessed by the Lord, and it was given to the husband and wife before sin entered the world in Genesis 3. Thus, physical desire for intimacy is not an evil desire; it is God-given.

However, after the fall, when Adam and Eve sinned against God, the consequences of sin affected all of creation, including God's design for human sexuality. And in response, throughout the whole Bible, God gives prohibitions and prescriptions for how He desires us to enjoy one another intimately under His creative design. God calls any physical intimacy or fulfillment of sexual desire that goes against His created order sexual immorality. Thus, the worldly way of thinking about physical intimacy is a distortion of God's design and intention going all the way back to the creation order in Genesis.

God's Prohibition

There are a number of passages in the Scriptures we could examine, but we are going to take a look at a few that I believe are vital for you to embrace. The Bible regards sexual sin as a unique sin against God's creation. Here is an important passage by the Apostle Paul to the Corinthian church when he had to address an issue of immorality.

> **"Flee sexual immorality! Every other sin a person commits is outside the body, but the person who is sexually immoral sins against his own body. Don't you know that your body is a temple of the Holy Spirit who is in you, whom you have from God? You are not your own, for you were bought at a price. So glorify God with your body."**
> **1 Corinthians 6:18-20 (CSB)**

The command is to flee sexual immorality. Do not play around with it. Do not take this issue lightly. You may read this passage and think that all evil and sin people commit is done with some part of their body. However, what this passage highlights is the nature of humanity being created in the image of God, in His likeness. Our sexuality as humans is based in our personhood. Physical intimacy is a unique union between image bearers of God. Thus, sexual immorality is a direct offense to God's design. God has bought you with a price since Jesus Christ paid for your sins by dying on the cross. Now, you are to glorify God with your body, which in reality is actually His body now. In other words, I want you to remember that you belong to the Lord. It is not about me and what I think. It is not even about your parents and what they think. It is about you and the Lord, and what the Lord has for you. I want you to embrace the truth that you belong to Him. You are tailor-made for His glory.

Here is another important truth when it comes to God's will for your sexuality and following Jesus Christ. Many people ask the question, "What is God's will for my life?" Well, here you go:

> **"For this is God's will, your sanctification: that you keep away from sexual immorality, that each of you knows how to control his own body in holiness and honor, not with lustful passions, like the Gentiles, who don't know God. This means one must not transgress against and take advantage of a brother or sister in this manner, because the Lord is an avenger of all these offenses, as we also previously told and warned you. For God has not called us to impurity but to live in holiness. Consequently, anyone who**

rejects this does not reject man, but God, who gives you his Holy Spirit."

1 Thessalonians 4:3-8 (CSB)

We find here that a major part of your sanctification—your growth into becoming more like Jesus—is directly connected to you avoiding sexual immorality. This means that you exercise self-control over all of your bodily urges. Your body does not control you, but rather you control your body. Remember, self-control is part of the fruit of the Spirit.[3] By faith in Jesus Christ, you have been given the capacity for self-control by the power of the Holy Spirit living in you.

We are reminded of this fact because this passage compares those in Christ who walk in sanctification—avoiding sexual immorality—to the "Gentiles, who do not know God." This is a strong way of saying that sexual immorality is the lifestyle of those who do not have a personal relationship with God, and does not belong in the life of the believer. The text ends with a strong declaration: the one who rejects this command does not reject a particular man or woman, does not reject an opinion or belief, but rather rejects the very God who created us, saves us, and gives His Holy Spirit to us.

God's Prescription

Since God has given us stern warnings and strong commands to avoid sexual immorality, how are we supposed to live out the physical intimacy He has designed for us? Here is an important passage for you to understand God's intention for physical intimacy.

> **"Marriage is to be honored by all and the marriage bed kept undefiled, because God will judge the sexually immoral and adulterers."**
>
> **Hebrews 13:4 (CSB)**

This verse teaches the honor and distinction of the marriage union between husband and wife. The marriage bed represents not only the physical intimacy shared between husband and wife, but also God's intention that the marital union remains pure. The Lord is opposed to any and all sexual activities that are outside the parameters of His design and intent for husband and wife. Unfortunately, the worldly way of thinking has distorted our view of the excitement, joy, and security God intends for physical intimacy in marriage.

> **"Now in response to the matters you wrote about: 'It is good for a man not to have sexual relations with a woman.' But because**

sexual immorality is so common, each man
should have sexual relations with his own
wife, and each woman should have sexual
relations with her own husband. A husband
should fulfill his marital duty to his wife,
and likewise a wife to her husband. A wife
does not have the right over her own body,
but her husband does. In the same way, a
husband does not have the right over his own
body, but his wife does. Do not deprive one
another—except when you agree for a time,
to devote yourselves to prayer. Then come
together again; otherwise, Satan may tempt
you because of your lack of self-control."

1 Corinthians 7:1-5 (CSB)

Again, this passage says to avoid sexual immorality. The passage starts by saying that abstinence is a good thing. However, God created marriage as the perfect place for the gift of sex to be enjoyed between a husband and a wife to avoid sexual immorality. Even before the Fall in Genesis 3, God blessed and gave humanity physical intimacy between a husband and a wife for unification, procreation, and recreation, so that we do not fall into sin and follow Satan. It is a gift given by God so that we may enjoy all that God has provided and intended. Notice how physical intimacy is described as freely giving oneself to your spouse. The world views sex in a very selfish way—it is all about get,

get, get. However, God's design is to give, give, give so that the husband and wife fully enjoy one another in freedom and true intimacy.

I want you to follow and thrive in God's design. Trust the Lord! I do not want you to commit to God's design just because your church said so, or your pastor said so, or because your parents said so. No! I want you to commit to God's design because this is how the Lord has called you to live as a committed follower of Jesus Christ.

You may find yourself in a position where you are being tempted with sexual immorality. This is why your crowd, your closest friends, and even the person you have romantic feelings for should be people who encourage you to live for the Lord. You all should encourage one another to abstain and avoid sexual immorality, and reserve yourself to live under God's design in holy matrimony.

Temptation will come. Satan tempted Jesus in the wilderness, so do not think you will be free from temptation.[4] However, you should never fear the temptation from the enemy. Here are two important verses you need for overcoming temptation:

> **"No temptation has come upon you except what is common to humanity. But God is faithful; he will not allow you to be tempted beyond what you are able, but with the**

temptation he will also provide the way out
so that you may be able to bear it."

1 Corinthians 10:13 (CSB)

"No one undergoing a trial should say, 'I
am being tempted by God,' since God is
not tempted by evil, and he himself doesn't
tempt anyone."

James 1:13 (CSB)

These two verses should be a huge encouragement to
you. 1 Corinthians 10:13 tells you that you are not alone in
facing temptation, because all of us face temptation. Not
only that, but in any temptation you face in life, the Lord
provides you with a way of escape. God will provide you
an open door to flee, but you must have already made up
your mind to run through that door.

Additionally, James 1:13 tells you that the temptations in
your life do not come from God. God is not tempted by any
evil and thus He tempts no man or woman. Temptation is
from the devil himself in order to entice you to sin against
God. So, when you face temptation, know that it is from the
enemy of God, and remember that the Lord will provide a
way out. Pray and look for that way out, and when you see
it, take it!

Protect yourself! You have to protect your ears and eyes.
You have to pay attention to what you are listening to and

watching. Do not watch things on your computer, laptop, TV, tablet, or phone that are sexually immoral. You have to put those things away because of what those things do to your mind. They stir up the sin nature, and they take you down a path that you never thought you would be on. Watch your ears. This is why Jesus uses such strong language in condemning adultery:

> **"If your right eye causes you to sin, tear it out and throw it away. For it is better that you lose one of your members than that your whole body be thrown into hell. And if your right hand causes you to sin, cut it off and throw it away. For it is better that you lose one of your members than that your whole body go into hell."**
>
> **Matthew 5:29-30 (CSB)**

Jesus uses hyperbole to prove a point of how important it is for you to avoid sin. He says it is better for you to lose a limb than for you to lose your whole body to destruction in eternal separation from God. If your friends are encouraging you to look at pornography or encouraging you to commit sexually immoral acts, they are not acting as true friends. If the person you have romantic feelings for is encouraging you to compromise your faith by going against God's design of sexual intimacy between a husband and a wife, they are not acting in love. Stand firm in your commitment to Christ Jesus, and He will give you the strength and all you need to walk in victory.

Conclusion

You matter. Your crowd matters. Your relationships matter. Your romantic relationships matter. And remember, all of this goes back to your value in God's eyes. Your Creator has made you. You have been remarkably, amazingly, awesomely, wonderfully, and fearfully made with a plan and purpose directly from God. Therefore, surround yourself with Christlike people so that you can encourage one another to live for the glory of Jesus Christ.

You may be in a situation where it is difficult to find friends who are committed to following Jesus Christ. You may be surrounded by youth who do not go to church, who do not believe the Bible, or who do not believe in Jesus Christ. Or you may be surrounded by peers who say they believe in the Bible or in Jesus, but the way they live shows they do not care about living for Jesus. Here is what you should do:

Time and Access
Limit the time you spend with them and the access you give them to your life, so that they do not corrupt your walk with Jesus.

Commitment
Be a loving and caring Christian witness to your peers by showing them your commitment to Jesus. Who knows, God may have you in their lives so that those peers come to know Jesus for themselves.

Pray
Pray that God brings people into your life who love Him and want to honor Him as they live out their faith.

These close relationships in your life as a youth play a key role in your current kingdom development. You will be amazed at how God will put brothers and sisters in Christ in your life in ways you never expected.

Self-Reflection

1. How have your friends helped you or hurt you in your commitment to live for Jesus?

2. How have you helped your friends make good decisions in living for Jesus?

3. How have you responded to temptation in regard to sexual immorality?

4. What are some things you will start doing today to avoid sexual immorality and to live in purity for the Lord until marriage?

5. How will you cultivate friendships and romantic relationships that honor and give glory to God?

Chapter 5

Your Development

In sports, there is a very important time of the year known as off-season training. This kind of training occurs months before the season even starts. It is during this time of year where development and growth takes place, and champions are made. Athletes work hard to get stronger, faster, and in better physical condition. As the season approaches, the teams then go into training camps. Training camps transition athletes from off-season training to more focused and specific preparation for the team just before the season begins. They continue to condition their bodies and minds, while also implementing the playbook they will run during the season. They train, develop, and try to become the best they can be once the season starts.

We not only see this in sports but also in marching bands. Before the school year starts, the bands meet early in the mornings to practice and get ready for the season. They also go through camp so they can be ready for the show.

I want you to see the years of your youth in a similar manner. You are undergoing development and training. Do not think this part of your life is insignificant. Do not take this stage of your life for granted. In order to be all that God has called you to be you must undergo development and training. Check out how important growth and development truly is in God's plan for your life. Luke 2:40-52 shows us Jesus' maturation and says that He grew in stature, wisdom, and favor with man and God. This goes to show that Jesus, the Son of God incarnate, God in the flesh, fully God and yet as being fully man, also grew and developed.

This is the time of your life for you to develop and grow. Do not waste this time. Do not mock or push aside all of the things that God is placing in front of you. For you to mature and do all that God has purposed for your life, your development is crucial. In the previous chapter we looked at the four Hebrew youth: Daniel, Hananiah, Mishael and Azariah. As youth, they decided to make some major decisions for the Lord. As they made these decisions to live for the Lord, I find it so interesting that God kept Daniel in a position of leadership from his youth under King Nebuchadnezzar of Babylon, even into the reign of King Cyrus of the Medo-Persians. The leadership and authority given to Daniel as a youth extended into his old age. This all began when he made the decision to stand for the Lord as a youth.

See, Babylon was conquered by Medo-Persia, and they had new kings take over the land. But Daniel remained in his position and in charge because He served and trusted the Lord. And not just when he was young— Daniel continued to live for and trust in the Lord throughout his adult years. So much so, his political enemies even tried to kill

> **The development you go through in your youth, right now, is preparing you for amazing things the Lord has for you**

him because of his faith. But God protected him. From Daniel's youth, and all the way into his eighties, he was still running the show. Leadership changed all around him. People came, and people left, but Daniel remained in his position of influence calling shots because he trusted the Lord at an early age. He allowed the Lord to use that time to develop him. That catapulted him into his older years. The development you go through in your youth, right now, is preparing you for amazing things the Lord has for you, but sometimes this development can be very uncomfortable and even unexpected.

Uncomfortable Development

In Genesis 41, we find that Joseph was 30 years old when the Egyptian Pharaoh placed him in charge over all of Egypt, including Pharaoh's house. The Egyptian Pharaoh witnessed, firsthand, God's favor working in Joseph's life. God revealed to Joseph the answer to Pharaoh's disturbing dream that a famine would hit the land of Egypt and beyond, and Joseph gave Pharaoh the solution to save the people. Thus, Joseph became the man in charge over the entire nation, while Pharaoh basically took a long vacation from his normal responsibilities.

Now, you might think God working in Joseph's life and placing him in such a position of power came out of nowhere, but really, this journey started when Joseph was a youth. His preparation began in his own household, and it took many twists and turns that we would not wish on our worst enemies. His journey was rough, but Joseph's development prepared him for exactly what God had in store for him to do—namely, to bless and save a nation, along with his own family.

Joseph Betrayed

We are introduced to Joseph in Genesis 37 as a seventeen-year-old. He was Jacob's favorite son, and his older brothers did not like the favoritism that Joseph received from their father. In the midst of this tense family situation, Joseph received dreams about the call God placed on his life and what he would do. He had dreams of himself being in a elevated position and his entire family bowing down to him. Joseph's family did not like it. His own brothers betrayed him and planned to kill him until the eldest brother came up with the plan to sell Joseph into slavery instead of taking his life. Thus, Joseph, at age seventeen, was sold into slavery and was sent to Egypt.

Joseph Enslaved

In Genesis 39, as a slave in Egypt, the Lord was with Joseph and caused all Joseph did to prosper. Joseph was placed in charge over all of Potiphar's—the captain of the guard of Egypt—household and everything he owned. Unfortunately, even while walking in such favor from God, Potiphar's wife falsely accused Joseph of rape because he repeatedly refused to sleep with her—a decision he made because of his commitment to not sin against the Lord. Joseph took a stand for righteousness, but because Potiphar believed his wife's lie, Potiphar threw him into prison. Though Joseph was committed to the Lord, he went from being a trusted slave in Egypt to being a prisoner in Egypt. However, interestingly enough, Genesis 39 concludes that the Lord was still with Joseph and continued to bless him even in jail.

Joseph Imprisoned

In Genesis 40, Joseph is in prison for a crime he did not commit. He is innocent. However, the Bible continues to say that the Lord was with Joseph and continued to bless him. So again, Joseph was put in charge—this time over the whole prison. While in prison, Joseph exercised his God-given gift to interpret dreams. He correctly interpreted the dreams of Pharaoh's officials—the chief baker and chief cupbearer. Joseph asked the chief cupbearer to tell Pharaoh about him so that he could be released from unjust imprisonment. But just when you thought Joseph would finally be set free, the cupbearer forgot about Joseph.

Two more years passed by, and Pharaoh had two dreams that really troubled him, but no one in his court could interpret the dreams. It was then that the chief cupbearer remembered a prisoner named Joseph who correctly interpreted his dream when he was in prison. Pharaoh called for Joseph, and he correctly interpreted Pharaoh's dreams that there would be seven years of abundance in the land, followed by seven years of famine that would devastate the land and cause much suffering. But Joseph also gave Pharaoh the solution to the problem. By storing a fifth of the produce of the land during the seven years of abundance, Pharaoh could provide food to the people during the seven years of famine. It was then that Pharaoh

gave Joseph a wife and made him ruler over all of Egypt—
except for Pharaoh who sat on the throne.

Joseph Saved

Joseph, as ruler of Egypt, stockpiled food during the
seven years of abundance for the following seven years of
famine. The famine in the land grew severe and reached
into Canaan. Jacob and his family also needed food, so he
sent ten of his sons who had sold Joseph into slavery to
Egypt to purchase food. Not knowing it was their brother,
they came face to face with Joseph to purchase food.
Joseph tested them to prove their sincerity. Through this,
the brothers acknowledged and owned their past sins
against their long-lost brother Joseph. In dramatic fashion,
Joseph revealed himself to his brothers as their long-lost
brother. Even in his great power he showed his brothers
forgiveness and compassion. Joseph brought his father
Jacob (aka Israel) and the entire family to live in Egypt and
gave them all the best the country had to offer. God used
Joseph to save Egypt, the surrounding lands, and his own
family from calamity.

One of the most important verses in all of the Bible is
found in Joseph's speech to his brothers.

**"You planned evil against me; God planned
it for good to bring about the present result—
the survival of many people."**

Genesis 50:20 (CSB)

God strategically placed Joseph in the right place, at
the right time, to be the right answer to Egypt's and the
surrounding region's problem. Through the betrayal of his
brothers, the lies from Potiphar's wife, and being forgotten
in prison, God was developing Joseph. And remember, this
process started when Joseph was seventeen years old. It
took thirteen long years for him to come to power in Egypt.
In his journey to the top, he was developed administratively
as he ran the household and affairs of the Egyptian official,
Potiphar. When he was thrown into prison, he was further
developed as he ran the entire Egyptian prison. Joseph
learned the language, the culture, and the inner workings
of Egyptian society for the purpose that God was preparing
him to fulfill.

This administrative development in Egypt, along with
the wisdom and the gifting by the Holy Spirit that God
gave to Joseph, enabled him to save lives. All of that began
back when he was a youth, a teenager. He did not decide to
wait until he was a certain age to begin living his life for the
Lord. Joseph remained committed to God and exercised
his God-given gifts in the most uncomfortable situations

which ultimately developed and prepared him for his destiny to lead and save a nation.

Unexpected Development

Not only can your development as a youth towards your destiny be uncomfortable, but it can be very much unexpected. *The Karate Kid* was one of the most popular movies of the 1980s—so much that they made four sequels, a reboot almost thirty years later, and a series produced by Netflix called *Cobra Kai* that continues the original story. In the original movie, a teenager named Daniel moves to a new neighborhood and school. The experience becomes horrific as a group of teenagers who know karate begin beating him up. One day as Daniel is being beaten, an elderly gardener, Mr. Miyagi, jumps in and fights off all the teenagers. Daniel learns that Mr. Miyagi is also an old martial arts master and asks him to teach him karate.

Miyagi agrees, but for weeks, he simply makes Daniel sand the floors a particular way, paint fences in a specific manner, and wash and wax cars in a peculiar way. Daniel gets so frustrated because weeks and weeks have gone by, and he is basically Miyagi's servant. He thought he was there to learn karate.

In an iconic scene, Daniel lashes out at Mr. Miyagi in frustration. How does Mr. Miyagi respond? He throws various punches and kicks at Daniel. Daniel, instinctively, blocks every punch and kick using all the movements and motions he learned from sanding floors, painting fences, and waxing cars. All that mundane work built his strength and taught him defensive karate techniques. Daniel had been trained and developed to defend himself without even knowing it.

It is one thing for you to be developed and trained for a job or position on purpose. Then you know what you should focus on so that you can be successful. It is quite another thing to be developed and trained and have no idea it is happening. King David is the most popular and honored kings of the nation of ancient Israel. Yet, he is probably most known for defeating the giant, Goliath, with a simple slingshot (1 Samuel 17). Oh and by the way, he was a young teenager when he did this. However, we often fail to realize that David's success in experiencing God's promises by defeating the nation of Israel's enemies did not go back to David's defeat of Goliath, but rather when he was a young shepherd boy.

The Bible introduces David as a youth when God places a call on his life. Due to King Saul's repeated disobedience, God told the prophet Samuel that He had chosen another king to take Saul's place.[1] God sent Samuel out, but Samuel did not know exactly who He was looking for.

When Samuel arrived at Jesse's house, Jesse presented seven sons to Samuel, but God said it was none of them. Jesse did not even consider his son David capable of being king. Yet God had other plans. The other sons looked capable, but God looks at the heart. Even though David would not assume the throne until many years later, Samuel anointed the young shepherd boy as king of Israel—and note, David was a youth, possibly even a pre-teen.[2]

Understanding David's call on his life is important to fully grasp how God works in the life of His people. See, when David fought the giant, Goliath, to defend the nation of Israel against the Philistines, David's confidence came from a history he had with the Lord years before as a shepherd boy.

During this time, David served King Saul as an assistant. When David heard the giant, Goliath, defying the armies of Israel, he was offended and volunteered to fight—even though he was not old enough to fight in Israel's army. King Saul listed several reasons why David was not able to fight Goliath. I love David's response:

> **"David answered Saul, 'Your servant has been tending his father's sheep. Whenever a lion or a bear came and carried off a lamb from the flock, I went after it, struck it down,**

**and rescued the lamb from its mouth. If it
reared up against me, I would grab it by its
fur, strike it down, and kill it. Your servant
has killed lions and bears; this uncircumcised
Philistine will be like one of them, for he has
defied the armies of the living God.' Then
David said, 'The Lord who rescued me
from the paw of the lion and the paw of the
bear will rescue me from the hand of this
Philistine.'"**

1 Samuel 17:34-37 (CSB)

David's confidence in that moment to defeat this giant,
who had the entire army of Israel terrified, came from his
development and training as a shepherd boy protecting the
sheep for which he was responsible. As a shepherd, David
was responsible to feed the sheep, keep the sheep together,
and protect them from predators. David told Saul that as
a young shepherd boy, at different times, a lion and a bear
took one of the sheep. David went after that lion and that
bear, grabbed them by the fur and struck both of them
down, bringing the sheep back to the flock safely.

You see, David realized that he was ready for the moment
against Goliath because he already had a history of battle
success. David was trained to fight, not through military
training, but rather as a young boy protecting sheep. Surely
someone who grabbed a hungry lion or a bear by the fur

and killed them to rescue one sheep among all the others was ready to face a mere man.

Please do not miss the most important part of David's history though. David's confidence was not just because he had battle experience. His confidence came from his history with God in those moments. David realized that God was the one who gave him those victories against the lion and the bear, and that it was not because of his own power and strength. The same was true with Goliath. Even though David was developed and trained during his years as a shepherd, ultimately, David's confidence came from placing his trust in the Lord. And those experiences as a youth prepared him to place all his confidence in the Lord when he would become king of Israel. His training and preparation involved him learning to take responsibility fully for what was placed in his charge and to trust God to be able to take care of his responsibilities.

The story of David's life as a youth is just for you. God has given you responsibilities at this time in your life. They may seem like they are insignificant. They may seem pointless, boring, and a waste of time. But trust me, God has you where you are and has given you the responsibilities and opportunities you have

Embrace these years of your youth as development, training, and preparation

right now to develop and train you for the call He has on your life. God wants you to develop a history of trusting Him now in your youth, so that when you are older, your confidence in the Lord remains strong.

Conclusion

Youth Matter! God wants to show you even now that He can be trusted to develop and prepare you with what you need in order to accomplish what He has for you in this life. It does not matter what opposition, enemies, or giants that come against you. God wants to show you that He is faithful and that He has you in the palm of His hand. God has your back at a level that you cannot imagine right now, and He wants you to trust Him.

Therefore, God will allow you to be placed in situations where the only thing you can do is trust Him and lean on Him. Now this does include utilizing what you have. God equips you with certain gifts, talents, and abilities, and skills, but those are nothing unless He steps in and empowers those abilities to accomplish things that you could not do on your own.

You must be constantly learning and growing in Christ Jesus. Just because you win one battle, does not mean another one is not just around the corner. Remember, Satan left Jesus after tempting Him in the wilderness, but sought another "opportune time."[3] Embrace these years of your youth as development, training, and preparation. The tough times that you face are times that God is growing you. Fine-tune and hone the skills and abilities you have now and pray that God shows you how to use them. Pray that He also shows up when you use them. And, when the time comes to go to another level as you mature and grow, you will experience God in a way that will bring all glory to His name.

Self-Reflection

1. How do you view challenges and hard times in life right now?

2. What have you learned about yourself when facing challenging situations?

3. What do you think God may be preparing you for in life?

4. How will you begin viewing this time of development in your life?

Chapter 6

Your Impact

As you discovered in the previous chapter, your development as a youth is critical for the future God has for you. However, God's plan for your life is not only about development for the future, but also the potential for you to have an impact right now. When I was growing up, there was an old saying: "Why put off for tomorrow what can be done today?" You do not have to wait until you reach your twenties, thirties, forties, or fifties to serve the Lord and make an impact for the Kingdom of God. You can do it right now!

By embracing the truth that *Youth Matter*, you can impact your family and community for the cause of Christ in ways you have never imagined. While it is true that you are in a stage of development and preparation, even right now, God can and will do some major things in and through you for His kingdom. One of my favorite Scriptures about the impact you can have in your youth says,

> **"Let no one despise you for your youth, but set the believers an example in speech, in conduct, in love, in faith, in purity."**
>
> **1 Timothy 4:12 (ESV)**

The Apostle Paul wrote these words to a young Timothy because Paul set Timothy in a position of authority. One of his responsibilities included preparing and appointing leaders in the church. While it is likely that Timothy was not a teenager, Timothy was still very young to serve in such a leadership position and was likely not taken seriously because of his age. The Apostle Paul encouraged Timothy to not allow himself to be taken for granted but rather to serve as an example to all the people, including his elders, of what it looks like to follow Jesus. The Bible gives us many other examples of youth stepping up and making an impact for the mission of God. Let's look at a couple of historical figures that demonstrate what it looks like for youth to set an example and have kingdom impact despite their young age.

Youth in Leadership

In 2 Kings 22–23 and 2 Chronicles 34–35, there was a king named Josiah who began his rule in Jerusalem at eight years old. Yes, you read that correctly. He was eight years old and sat on the throne as king of the southern kingdom of Judah. Not only that, but he reigned for thirty-one years. Josiah did great and mighty things for the Lord, but he did not wait until he was an adult to serve the Lord. He started as a child, and continued serving the Lord as a youth, and into adulthood. During the eighth year of his reign, when he was approximately fifteen or sixteen years old, he sought out the Lord regarding what kind of king he should to be. Josiah desired to be a godly king, wanting to follow in the footsteps of King David. Because of this, he removed the idolatry—the worshipping and serving of false gods— that was running rampant in the land. He tore down the pagan places of worship and reinstituted the true worship of the Lord. Josiah cleansed the Lord's temple, and during the process, the priests found the book of the Law!

Now you may be wondering why I put an exclamation point at the end of that last sentence. What was so important about the cleansing of the temple? Why make a big deal out of finding the book of the Law? Why are we talking about Josiah reestablishing proper worship of the Lord? Well here is a quick, yet important, history lesson. You see, God told the nation of Israel that He was giving them the Promised Land when He delivered them from slavery in Egypt. He made a covenant with Israel with conditions that they were to obey Him in order to remain in the Promised Land. The Lord told them that if they broke His covenant and walked in the sins of the nations that were previously there, He would cast them out of the land as well.[1]

When Josiah first became king at the age of eight, the kingdom was full of idol worship and evil practices due to the ungodly leadership of the previous kings. The people followed that ungodly leadership and disregarded God's Word, both in their religious worship and their daily behavior in living for the Lord. Thus, during the reign of Josiah, removing the idolatrous pagan places of worship, cleansing the temple of God for proper worship, and finding the book of the Law were important so that the people could know exactly what the Lord required of them. By knowing what the Lord expected and obeying His expectations, they would not be kicked out of the land as discipline from the Lord.

On top of that, how absurd is it that they lost the book of the Law in the first place? Think about that. The book of the Law was supposed to remain in the temple so that the priests could operate from it. The priests and scribes were responsible for teaching God's laws from this book to the people. The book of the Law was so important that God gave careful instructions to the king concerning it:

> "Now it shall come about when he sits on
> the throne of his kingdom, he shall write for
> himself a copy of this law on a scroll in the
> presence of the Levitical priests. It shall be
> with him and he shall read it all the days of
> his life, that he may learn to fear the Lord his
> God, by carefully observing all the words of
> this law and these statutes, that his heart may
> not be lifted up above his countrymen and
> that he may not turn aside from the
> commandment, to the right or the left, so that
> he and his sons may continue long in his
> kingdom in the midst of Israel."
>
> Deuteronomy 17:18-20 (NASB95)

Additionally, look at what God says to Joshua about the book of the Law:

> "This book of the law shall not depart from
> your mouth, but you shall meditate on it day
> and night, so that you may be careful to do
> according to all that is written in it; for then
> you will make your way prosperous, and
> then you will have success."
>
> Joshua 1:8 (NASB95)

The book of the Law was so important to the lifeline of the Israelites. But how does something so important get lost? Well, the kings and priests stopped caring. They stopped fearing the Lord. They stopped meditating on it day and night. And eventually, over time, the book of the Law was lost in the temple of God.

This is happening in some places today. Think about how absurd it is for so many churches around the country to operate apart from the Bible; how many preachers preach without opening up the Bible; how many pastors pastor without consulting God's holy Word.

The book of the Law was lost in the very place that it was supposed to be, in the temple. But God used a young teenage king to turn a whole nation back to worshipping the true God, the creator of the heavens and the earth. A whole nation was impacted by a youth who made the decision to trust and obey the Lord. Josiah did not wait until he was an old man, but rather, Josiah started his mission in turning a nation back to God as a youth.

Youth Courage

In the previous chapter, we discussed David's development and preparation in his youth to be a great king in Israel's history. However, David's youth was not just about his development and preparation alone, but he also made a huge impact for the kingdom. As said before, David was a teenager when he stepped up to fight the giant, Goliath.

According to Numbers 1:3, you had to be at least twenty years old to fight in Israel's army. David had gone to serve King Saul as a youth after the prophet Samuel anointed the young David to be the next king.[2] Remember, David had seven older brothers, and at least three of them had reached twenty years old, so that they served in the army at the time Goliath challenged Israel.[3] Thus, some think David might have been a fourteen to sixteen-year-old shepherd boy at that time. This explains the responses David received from the soldiers and King Saul when he wanted to fight Goliath.

Because of David's age and his assumed lack of experience, King Saul had no confidence in David fighting the giant, Goliath. Moreover, Goliath felt extremely disrespected that it was a young boy and not an experienced soldier who accepted his challenge to fight. Now it is important to remember what all was at stake in this fight. In ancient battles, there were times in which instead of having entire armies fight one another, the armies would choose a "champion" from each army to fight as a representative of their respective armies. Whichever champion won the fight, meant a win for his respective army and nation.

In 1 Samuel 17, Goliath presented himself as the Philistine champion and whoever fought him, the loser's nation would bow and serve the winner's nation. All of Israel was scared to fight the giant because of his humongous size and his ginormous battle weapons. King Saul, who the Bible describes as one of the tallest men in Israel, was even terrified of Goliath.[4] King Saul was so afraid that he vowed to give whoever defeated Goliath a reward—riches, a princess for a wife, and no more taxes for the winner's family. That sounds like a pretty sweet deal, right? But still, nobody would step up to fight Goliath.

That is until David showed up. David was not even supposed to be there. He was simply bringing some food and supplies to his brothers who were serving in the army. Upon arriving, David saw how scared the army was of Goliath, so he asked what the reward was for defeating that giant who disrespected and disgraced Israel. When King Saul heard about this, he wanted to meet David, and when they met, David told him,

> **"Don't let anyone be discouraged by him; your servant will go and fight this Philistine!"**
> **1 Samuel 17:32 (CSB)**

Don't you love the confidence of this teenager? All the grown, military-trained men were terrified of the giant. But this youngster stepped up and basically said, "Don't worry about him. I'll take him off your hands." King Saul could not believe what he heard and told David there was no way he could win because Goliath had basically been a champion longer than David had even been alive. Not only was the giant, Goliath, too big for David, but he also had too much experience as well.

And it is right here that we see David understood something that King Saul did not. David's confidence did not rest in his own power or ability, but rather in the Lord's faithfulness. Let's look at David's words closely after he recounted his history of development and preparation with the Lord as a young shepherd boy guarding his father's sheep.

> **"Your servant has killed lions and bears; this uncircumcised Philistine will be like one of them, for he has defied the armies of the living God. Then David said, 'The Lord who rescued me from the paw of the lion and the paw of the bear will rescue me from the hand of this Philistine.' Saul said to David, 'Go, and may the Lord be with you.'"**
> **1 Samuel 17:36-37 (CSB)**

When David called the giant, Goliath, an "uncircumcised Philistine," David was appealing to God's covenant relationship and promises to Israel,[5] as well as God's anointing of David to be the next king of Israel. David's boldness and courage to fight against the giant was because He believed God's promises more than just his own abilities. He already built a history with the Lord defeating lions and bears. Surely, one who was not part of the covenant promises of God and one who defied the armies of the living God—thus defying God Himself—would not win.

King Saul tried to give David the king's armor, but it was too big and would not fit. So, David went out with what he already had and was used to using, his slingshot. David approached the giant, Goliath, without hesitation or fear. For David, this was more than a human battle; it was clearly just as much a spiritual battle. Goliath was not only offended that the Israelite army sent out a youngster to face him, but they sent out a youngster armed with only a slingshot! Goliath cursed David by his own pagan gods and basically told David he was about to die. But David replied with these famous words:

> "You come against me with a sword, spear, and javelin, but I come against you in the name of the Lord of Armies, the God of the ranks of Israel—you have defied him. Today, the Lord will hand you over to me. Today, I'll strike you down, remove your head, and give the corpses of the Philistine camp to the birds of the sky and the wild creatures of the earth. Then all the world will know that Israel has a

God, and this whole assembly will know that it is not by sword or by spear that the Lord saves, for the battle is the Lord's. He will hand you over to us."

1 Samuel 17:45-47 (CSB)

David ran to the battle line quickly, drew one smooth stone from his bag, hurled it from his slingshot, and struck the giant, Goliath, right between the eyes. And just in case anyone thought he was lying, David walked up, took Goliath's sword, and chopped off the giant's head. From there, the Israelite army overtook the Philistine army, and David became a great war-hero. While being a youth—a teenager—David made a huge impact for his entire nation because he used his development and preparation in the Lord in a time of great need.

> **Your peers, your friends, and even the adults around you need to see you live out this example of commitment to Jesus Christ**

Conclusion

Having kingdom impact has no age restrictions. Jesus does not want you to think that He cannot use you in mighty ways right now as a youth. Do not view your life now as the time to only "have fun" or "get everything out of your system." Do not think that you have to wait until you are older to fulfill the purpose and plan God has for you. He wants the closest of relationships with you right now, as a youth. He wants you to trust Him and depend on Him as He uses you for His glory!

We started this chapter talking about how God wants to use you as a youth right now to set an example of what it means to trust Him. We all need examples to follow. Textbooks and online lessons give examples of how to do the work. When we go to work, we get examples and demonstrations of what we are to do in our position. Video games come with a tutorial to show us how to play the game. In athletics, examples are provided whether on the field, court, or in the film room of what the player is supposed to do. We all need examples in every sphere of life and especially in godly living.

Ultimately, we look to Jesus as our perfect example. But in turn, Jesus uses His people—people like you—to become examples of godly living as well. There is no age restriction. What would it look like for you to model and demonstrate what true commitment to Jesus Christ looks like in your speech, conduct, love, faith, and purity? What would it look like for you to set the example in your home, family, school, church, and community?

You can set an example in your speech by the words you speak and the words you type in text messages and on social media.

You can set an example in your conduct not only how you act and live when everything is good, but also how you react to others when things are not good, or you have been mistreated by others.

You can set an example in your love by not just loving the lovable, but even demonstrating love to those who do not deserve it.

You can set an example in faith by trusting and staying committed to the Lord when others around you think you should go a different direction.

You can set an example in purity by standing firm in your commitment to Jesus when others try to pressure you to go against the Word of God.

Your peers, your friends, and even the adults around you need to see you live out this example of commitment to Jesus Christ.

That is why I love the historical narrative of the four Hebrew youth we talked about in Chapter 3. Remember, because of four Hebrew youth who repeatedly displayed uncompromising faith in the Lord, Nebuchadnezzar came to recognize that the Lord was indeed the one true God.[6] God wants to use you the same way. You can make this kind of impact right now in your life.

You do not have to wait. Your parents may be waiting on you to be that example, and they do not even know it. Your teachers may be waiting on you to be that example, and they do not even know it. The people in your community may be waiting on you as a teenager, or you as a pre-teen, to see the example of what it really means to know and trust the Lord and exemplify Christlike living. Let's make that impact now!

Self-Reflection

1. When have you had an opportunity to encourage others to trust God's Word?

2. When have you had to lean on your personal history with the Lord for courage to continue going?

3. What are some ways that you can be an example right now in your speech, in conduct, in love, in faith, and in purity?

Chapter 7

Your Growth

There are state fair contests all over the country where farmers bring in giant fruits or vegetables to be weighed and measured. The farmer who brings the largest and heaviest vegetable or fruit is declared the winner and receives thousands of dollars. You may have seen this on television where they even have to use a forklift to pick up and transport a watermelon, a squash, a potato, or a pumpkin. I have often wondered how they grow the food to be so big. Then I found out that there were some intentional things done to encourage and promote such growth in order to reach those ginormous sizes. The farmers use special kinds of fertilizer, feed, and strategic lighting. The farmers even have a specific kind of watering schedule to promote optimal growth and development. All-in-all, these foods do not grow to those humungous sizes by luck or chance. It does not just happen. There is intentional, strategic, committed work that produces these amazing results.

The same is true when it comes to your growth in Christ Jesus. There is an old saying that goes something like this, "Jesus did not come to make bad people good, but to make dead people live." As Ephesians 2:10 explains, Jesus saved you so that you can truly live the life He has planned for you. One thing that is true in this physical life, where there is life there is growth. Life does not remain stagnant, it is either moving, growing, and developing or it is dying. This is especially true when it comes to growing your relationship with the Lord. There is always room to grow in your walk with Christ.

I am speaking specifically about spiritual growth. Too often we as believers fall into the trap of thinking that God is only concerned with us saying yes to Jesus and trusting Him for the forgiveness of our sins. Yes, by placing faith in the finished work of Christ—His life, death, burial, resurrection, ascension, and His sending of the Holy Spirit—we are saved from our sins so that we may have eternal life. We say yes, and we are saved, but we do not immediately die and go to heaven. We remain here, on earth. And Jesus has not come back yet as He said He would to set up His eternal kingdom. So, what are we supposed to be doing in the meantime?

There is a particular growth that God has designed for His people. This is a part of our purpose, and as the Holy Spirit is working in us, there are things that we do as well. There are practices, disciplines, and habits that you can do right now as a youth to promote and strengthen your growth in the Lord. This is the exact thing that Paul celebrated in the opening of his letter to the Colossian church:

> **"For this reason also, since the day we heard this, we haven't stopped praying for you. We are asking that you may be filled with the knowledge of his will in all wisdom and spiritual understanding, so that you may walk worthy of the Lord, fully pleasing to him: bearing fruit in every good work and growing in the knowledge of God, being strengthened with all power, according to his glorious might, so that you may have great endurance and patience, joyfully giving thanks to the Father, who has enabled you to share in the saints' inheritance in the light. He has rescued us from the domain of darkness and transferred us into the kingdom of the Son he loves. In him we have redemption, the forgiveness of sins."**
> **Colossians 1:9-14**

The Apostle Paul continually prayed that the Colossian church would grow in spiritual maturity. He prayed for it and celebrated spiritual growth. This spiritual maturity would be the result of being filled with the knowledge of God's will. This means that they would know what God thinks and desires for them. This knowledge consists of all wisdom and spiritual understanding. Thus, it is not something learned or discovered by human standards, but rather given directly from God based on their trust and commitment to the Lord.

We must understand that the knowledge of God's will is not for the sake of knowing more information, but for the purpose of walking in a manner worthy of the Lord. We just read about four ways we walk in a worthy manner.

Bearing Fruit

The first is by bearing fruit. You can literally see fruit on a tree. Likewise, people should literally be able to see evidence of this growing knowledge of God's heart and mind when they observe our lifestyle.

Growing Knowledge of God

Second, we grow in the knowledge of God. This may seem redundant, and it is, somewhat. However, this is a bonus. As we grow in knowing God's Word, we grow in understanding God's ways.

Being Strengthened in the Lord

Third, we are strengthened in the Lord for the purpose that we exercise endurance and patience as we navigate the ups and downs of life. We do not lose heart and go into despair, but rather continue in Christlike confidence and hope.

Giving Thanks

And lastly, we live a life of thanksgiving, because we know the promises we have in Christ Jesus. Through the finished work of Jesus, the Father has rescued us from the dominion of darkness, and we have eternal life in the Kingdom of God.

The rest of this chapter discusses things that you can do to promote and encourage growth and spiritual maturity so that you can walk in your purpose, becoming more like Christ Jesus every single day. This list is not exhaustive, but these practices, disciplines, and habits can help you grow in kingdom development and kingdom impact.

Bible Study

The first place to start pursuing spiritual growth is to get in the Word of God. In order to know what God's will is, you must read what God has spoken. Thus, you must read and study the Bible. Here is why:

"All Scripture is inspired by God, and is profitable for teaching, for rebuking, for correcting, for training in righteousness, so that the man of God may be complete, equipped for every good work."
2 Timothy 3:16-17 (CSB)

"All Scripture" is inspired by God or rather God-breathed. This simply means that the content and information contained in "All Scripture" is God's message to us—not human ideas about God.[1] Scripture here is the written words that we call the Bible. It is the authoritative witness of God and His actions and words in creation and history. In Luke 24:44, Jesus declared that all of the Old Testament spoke of Him. Thus, Jesus regarded the thirty-nine books of the Old Testament to be authoritative.

Moreover, John 1:1-3 declares Jesus to be the Living Word of God. So, when Jesus said in John 16:12-15 that the Holy Spirit would instruct the apostles, even their writings became authoritative in the same way as the prophets of the Old Testament.[2] This is why reading and studying the whole Bible is so important. Through it, we get to know the will of God.

Studying the Bible offers some amazing benefits to your growth. "All Scripture" is profitable for teaching, rebuking, correction, and training in righteousness. This means that as you engage God's Word, it will pay off in your life.

All Scripture teaches you truth.

All Scripture rebukes by showing you what is wrong in your life or with things around you.

All Scripture corrects by showing you how to make the wrong things right, including your own behavior.

All Scripture trains you in righteousness by showing you how to progressively live more like Christ.

Additionally, "All Scripture" produces a complete follower of Jesus that is equipped to live out God's purposes. God determines what is good and right, and how one ought to live, not the culture or society. Thus, your trust in and application of God's Word will produce in and out of us the life God has intended us to live.

The ultimate goal of "All Scripture" is so that we may know Jesus Christ and the salvation found in Him alone by faith alone. The Bible instructs us in how to live *for* God in this life so that we will live *with* God for all of eternity! Now, I know this can all sound intimidating at first. But I love to tell people, "If you can read and understand a text message from your friend, you can read and understand the Bible—God's text message to you." It is true that there are best practices and development in learning to study the Bible well, but this all starts with a commitment to reading it.[3]

Youth seeking to develop and make impact for the Kingdom of God must strive to grow in knowing God more deeply, to understand and know His will, so that you walk out the life He has purposed for you. Find a Bible reading plan from your church or online and commit to reading through the Bible daily. I also encourage you to read a chapter a day from Proverbs. Whatever day of the month it is that day, read that particular chapter of Proverbs. It will bless your life tremendously.[4] It does not matter whether you read in the morning, afternoon, evening, or before bed. Just read God's Word, whatever works best for you. Get in the Bible, and study it!

Prayer

Your prayer life is vitally important, too. If you want to grow in spiritual maturity, you must embrace the spiritual discipline of prayer. Prayer is your direct line of communication with God, the creator of the universe. Jesus continually taught His disciples how important it was to make prayer a lifestyle, and not a once in a while event. Also, understand that Christian prayer is not a monologue of you reciting scripted words at certain times of the day, or chanting, or babbling repeated words hoping you will be heard as Jesus stated in Matthew 6:7. Rather, Christian prayer is a dialogue with your Father in heaven. You speak to Him and through His Holy Spirit, He communicates back to you. Also, the power in your prayer is not found in your eloquence of speech, but in your dependence on God who answers prayer.

The Bible is full of different kinds of prayers and different expressions of prayer for different occasions. There are a few things to learn about how to develop your prayer life to become "good" at prayer.

Pray More

First, you can develop a mature prayer life by praying more. Like most things in life, the more you do something the better you get. Find a place where you can be alone or with minimal distractions. Jesus often went to a place to be alone to pray to the Father, and He even taught the disciples in Matthew 6:6 to go into a "private room" and pray to the Father in secret. This allows you to remove distractions so that you may focus on God.

Meditate on Scripture

Secondly, meditating on Scripture can strengthen your prayer life. As you meditate on God's Word, you can pray God's Word, His will, and His promises back to Him.

Pray With Others

Third, praying along with others—corporate prayer—develops your prayer life. Hearing others pray and praying for the needs of others alongside them strengthens your prayer life.

Read About Prayer

Lastly, reading about prayer helps develop your prayer life. This can be done by reading various prayers in the Old and New Testaments, as well as books and devotionals on prayer.

Christians pray to an audience of one—God! Therefore, you should speak truly from your mind and heart because God indeed knows what you need even before you ask, and He still expects you to pray. Therefore, you can pray in confidence that God hears you.[5] And not only does He hear you, but He answers.[6] God's answer is determined by His will and nature. To pray "in Jesus' name" is not like waving a magic wand, but rather it is to pray according to His revealed will and character.

Here are the three ways God answers: Yes, No, and Not Yet. God may give you a direct "yes" to your request. Sometimes that "yes" may come differently than you thought. God may say "no." If He says "no," then rejoice as well, because that means your request was not according to His will. Since He is good and faithful, being in His will is better than getting a "yes" outside of His will. Besides, maybe, just maybe, He has something better in store for you. The "not yet" answer is one of the hardest to handle. By nature, humans are impatient. However, in those times of waiting, you should remember that God's timing is perfect and that there is purpose in your waiting on God to fulfill what He is going to do.

Prayerlessness is a declaration of your independence from God. Meaning, when you do not communicate to God through prayer, you actually communicate to Him and to the watching world that you are just fine without Him. Do not give God the silent treatment. Talk to the Lord. Prayer is a dialogue, a conversation. Make it a lifestyle where you are constantly talking to the Lord, even if folks think you are weird and taking things too seriously. If and when you are questioned about your prayer life, use it as an opportunity to share your faith and pray for the person asking. Make it a lifestyle. Talk to God.

Worship

We often reduce worship to the time in a church service when we dance, shout, and sing to the Lord. However, worship is much more than that. To worship God is to ascribe the proper worth to God. It means to magnify His worthiness through praise and adoration, or to approach and address God as He is worthy. This can be done at a church gathering or privately. In a conversation with a Samaritan woman at the well, Jesus taught about the kind of worship the Father desires.

> **"But an hour is coming, and is now here, when the true worshipers will worship the Father in Spirit and in truth. Yes, the Father wants such people to worship him. God is spirit, and those who worship him must worship in Spirit and in truth."**
>
> **John 4:23-24 (CSB)**

Worship is not just about doing certain rituals, but rather, it is a heart and mind conditioned toward the worthiness of God in your behavior and lifestyle to honor Him, and only Him.[7] Worship often includes words and actions, but it goes beyond them to the focus of the mind and heart.[8] There is a sense in which all things done in obedience to the

Lord is worship, but these things are not substitutes for the direct worship of God.

Worship is a God-centered focus and response to God in His faithfulness. This kind of worship only occurs by faith in the person and work of Jesus Christ.[9] Jesus as the Messiah gives the Holy Spirit to all who place faith in Him as Lord and Savior. True worship is an expression of the indwelling of the Holy Spirit in the one who places faith in Jesus. Consequently, true worship only occurs when it is centered on Jesus Christ and empowered by the Holy Spirit.

Your worship, whether it is individual, or at a corporate church gathering is vitally important to your spiritual growth. Your faith and confidence in Christ grow the more you participate in worship services that are filled with prayer, songs of praise, the reading and teaching of the Word of God, and fellowship with other believers. Remember, singing and dancing counts as worship, but it is much more. Everything should be dedicated to showing how valuable and how worthy the Lord is in your life.

Service

Jesus was clear that He did not come to the world to be served, but to serve, and He gave his life as a ransom for many.[10] Jesus taught His disciples that greatness is found in serving, even in the most undesirable ways, and not ruling. He repeatedly displayed Himself as an example of the attitude and service that is expected in followers of the Christ.[11] Jesus is the supreme example of humility and servanthood, and true disciples of Jesus seek to learn from and do what Jesus has demonstrated. Here are a few motivations for serving the Lord:

Gratitude

First, serve out of *gratitude* for what the Lord has done for you.[12] It is not hard to serve the Lord when you truly consider all the great things He has done. He has made you, and through the atonement of Jesus Christ, you have forgiveness, the newness of life, and the promise of eternal salvation.

Love

Secondly, you are motivated to serve from *love*.[13] Your love for God and your love for your fellow neighbor motivates you to serve.

Obedience

Thirdly, you are motivated by *obedience*. As a child of the Most-High God you are commanded to serve. Obedience flows out of love. So, if you love God, you will obey His commands.[14]

Humility

And lastly, you are motivated by *humility*.[15] You serve from an understanding of who you are in Christ and how you are called to attend to the needs of others above your own.[16]

Having a heart to serve for the cause of Christ is work.[17] However, your labor in the Lord is not in vain. God remembers your work, and there will be rewards.[18] And while this can be hard work, it is not your strength that gets the job done, it is His.

God equips and empowers His children to serve Him as He sees fit. Believers are given spiritual gifts from the Holy Spirit to serve in the body of Christ.[19] Spiritual gifts are not the same as natural abilities and talents. These gifts are heightened special abilities given to the believer to glorify God for the purpose of service,[20] not for the purpose of showing off or thinking one is better than the other. If you belong to Christ, you have been gifted, and that gift is to be used to serve the Lord. You cannot work for, earn, or deserve these spiritual gifts. This truth should lead to humility, so that you do not think of yourself more highly than you ought.[21]

One of the best ways to discover and confirm which spiritual gift is yours is through serving in different capacities in the church. So, look for opportunities to serve in the church. From there, look for ways to serve in your community. But remember, we serve the community in the name of Jesus. This means that you do not serve and help out in order to earn respect or to be impressive and build a name for yourself. Rather, serve from a humble heart to put your love for Christ on display.

In fact, service is an act of worship. Therefore, do not be prideful, but rather serve and make it known that your service is for the Lord. Make it known that you are serving because you love Jesus, and you want people to understand and experience the love and joy of Jesus Christ. You do not serve because you have to, you serve because you get to!

Evangelism

Evangelism is a great way to grow in spiritual maturity. Normally when people hear the word evangelize, they feel fearful. It can be scary, but it is worth it. Evangelism is commanded in Matthew 28:19-20; Mark 16:15; Luke 24:47; John 20:21; Acts 1:8. Evangelism is simply sharing the Gospel of Jesus Christ. The word gospel means "good news." So, believers share the Good News of Jesus Christ to unbelievers so that they may trust in Jesus as their Lord and Savior for the forgiveness of their sins and have eternal life with Him.

Now some may think those commands were only for the original disciples. However, the command was to spread the gospel to the "ends of the earth," and Jesus being with them during this process to the "end of the age" shows that these commands went beyond the time of the Apostles. It was for all people who follow Jesus in all times.

Also, some think that evangelism is only the job for the evangelist, or the pastor, or the church staff.[22] However, we see throughout the New Testament that all believers are called to be a witness for Jesus.[23] This means that all believers are called to share the gospel. While every follower of Jesus Christ is not expected to use the same method of evangelism, every believer is expected to evangelize.

It is important to note that in the book of Acts, Jesus told the original Apostles to stay put until they received power—the Holy Spirit—to fulfill the command to take the gospel to the world.

> **"But you will receive power when the Holy Spirit has come on you, and you will be my witnesses in Jerusalem, in all Judea and Samaria, and to the ends of the earth."**
> **Acts 1:8 (CSB)**

It is good news that Jesus not only commands His followers to share the gospel, but He also empowers His people to do it! You do not rely on your own abilities or expertise, but the power of the Holy Spirit working in and through you. Your job in evangelism is to accurately deliver the message and to lean on the Holy Spirit to do only what He can do. The same power that the Holy Spirit used to save you is the same power that the Holy Spirit uses in you to share the Good News of Jesus Christ.

Please make special note that the gospel is a message and not just a lifestyle. Some people think living a good life alone is enough. This could not be further from the truth. It is true that your lifestyle of living like Jesus can open doors to share the gospel. However, living a good life or doing good deeds is not evangelism. Evangelism is sharing the message of Jesus Christ. So, just as doing good can open doors for people to listen to you to share the gospel, a lifestyle that contradicts the message of Jesus Christ can cause others to tune you out and not listen when you tell them about Jesus. Therefore, let your walk and talk match the message of Jesus Christ, the gospel.

> **If you understand that you belong to the Lord and that He saved you, then you know enough to tell somebody else**

Share your faith and make evangelism part of your lifestyle. Tell people how much you love the Lord. At school, on your athletic teams, school clubs, any and all extracurricular activities, tell people what the Lord has done for you. If you understand that your life is a gift and if you understand that you belong to the Lord and that He saved you, then you know enough to tell somebody else. This does not mean that you have to beat people over the head with the Bible, but rather part of your lifestyle is sharing your faith and the Good News of Jesus with others around you; the hope you have in Christ.

Few experiences are more exciting for a Christian than for God to use you as a follower of Jesus Christ to share the gospel with someone and that person accepts Jesus as Lord and Savior, and becomes a brother or sister in Christ! Nothing will fuel your faith more than telling people about your faith. This does not mean that everyone will believe. However, you will get more and more excited about your faith in Christ and what Christ is doing in your life the more you tell people about it.

Conclusion

This chapter began by stating how important spiritual growth is in the life of youth who know they matter. These practices, disciplines, and habits discussed are to be taken in a cumulative fashion.[24] Meaning, all of these spiritual disciplines work together, and when consistently engaged, they help produce Christlikeness in the life of all believers at every age. Your growth and maturation in Christ Jesus are a process. It is more like a marathon than a sprint. Therefore, be patient and consistent, and you will experience a peace and a joy in the Lord that you never imagined.

Self-Reflection

1. What are the steps you can take to make Bible study a daily routine?

2. On a scale of 1–10, where would you rate your prayer life? Why?

3. How much of a priority has intentional worship of God been in your life?

4. How often do you share the gospel on a weekly or monthly basis?

5. What are some steps that you will start today in sharing the Gospel of Jesus Christ with unbelievers?

6. What do you need to do to get started practicing these disciplines?

Chapter 8

Conclusion

I was moved by a story of a high school student who led many in his school to faith in Jesus Christ. Let's call this student Mike. He became a sort of spiritual leader for a group of Christians in his high school, and this movement became pretty popular. In response, a particular student club invited a guest speaker to teach against faith in Jesus as Lord and Savior. Mike found out and wanted to bring in another speaker to defend the Gospel of Jesus Christ. Since the opposing club went through the proper procedures under the school policies, Mike's group could not force that particular club to bring in another speaker for a debate. However, Mike found out that the speaker would allow questions to be asked at the end, so he made plans to attend.

Mike and his friends sat in the back of the meeting to hear the guest speaker talk about all the ways Jesus was not the Messiah and Savior of the world. Mike was impressed with how articulate and engaging the guest speaker was. At the conclusion of the presentation, Mike

You never know how God will use you as a youth for His glory!

began to ask the speaker a series of questions from the Bible. The guest speaker eloquently opposed each question with great skill. Mike went on and on, but at the end, Mike stopped, feeling as though he was out of his league in debating with this guest speaker.

Mike went on to become a Bible teacher, an author and guest lecturer. A little over thirty years later, Mike flew into a particular city to teach a Bible seminar. Before the lecture started, an older gentleman approached and sparked a conversation with Mike. Let's call this older gentleman Mr. Green. As they spoke Mike realized that Mr. Green was one of his former teachers at his old high school. Back then, Mr. Green was not a Christian, so when the seminar was over, Mike asked Mr. Green to share his testimony about how he came to faith in Jesus Christ.

Mr. Green told him years ago when he was still a high school teacher, one of the clubs brought in a guest speaker to talk about how Jesus is not the Messiah. Mr. Green said during that meeting a young student challenged the guest speaker with verse after verse, passage after passage,

Scripture after Scripture. Even though the guest speaker seemed to refute every claim, Mr. Green said his curiosity grew so much that he went to study those passages from the Bible for himself. It was through that study that he placed his faith in Jesus as Lord and Savior. Mr. Green then looked at Mike and said, "Any chance that you might know who that kid was who defended his faith in the club meeting." Mike looked at him, smiled in amazement, and said, "You are talking to him right now."[1] Mike learned that day how much *Youth Matter*. You never know how God will use you as a youth for His glory!

God Wants You

The goal of this book is to educate, equip, embolden, and encourage every youth who have placed faith in Jesus Christ as Lord and Savior. God is calling you to reject the amusement park youth mentality.[2] God wants to use you to lead by example, to demonstrate what it looks like for your generation to know, love, and serve the Lord.

It is an unfortunate reality that culture presents to youth the idea of a god that fits the desires of the culture. This god they create is, in fact, an idol, a false god, and no god at all. These new ideas of God have crept into some of our churches, and God is calling you to correct these false ideas about Him. The true God is not standing back at a distance, uninvolved in your life, and just hoping things go well with you. It is not God's main objective that you just be a good person, nor is His ultimate goal that you just be happy with your life.[3]

God as the creator of the heavens and the earth sees you as the crown of His creation. He is intimately involved in your life and wants you to experience Him in all that you do. He does not just want you to be a good person. He wants more. He wants an intimate relationship with you so that He can work through you to fulfill His mission and purposes in the earth. Moreover, the true God wants so much more for your life than happiness, because happiness is dependent on the things that happen around you. God wants you to have a constant experience of His joy that is found in your intimate relationship with Him, which is not dependent on what goes on around you.

I hope you now see that *Youth Matter*. You do not have to wait until you are older to let the Lord use you. It is really about understanding that you belong to the Lord. Embrace all the Lord has in store for you. This mindset is directly opposed to what many youth are told today. When I was a youth pastor, I started to get very frustrated when I heard people telling youth that they can be whatever they want to be. The common mantra is, "You can do whatever you put your mind to; whatever you can imagine or dream, you can do it." Let me tell you right now, that is the biggest lie anybody has ever told you because you cannot be whatever you want to be. You want to know why?

What if what you want to do, what you desire and set your mind to do with your life is something that God said no to? What do you do then? God says no and slams the door in your face. Now all of a sudden, you are mad at God because you have sought your will first and not His will. Many

> **It is not about what you want. It is about what God wants to do in and through you.**

people suffer frustrations in life because they have sought to do their own thing, and do not consider what the Lord has purposed and planned for their lives. Many people think they are fighting and battling against the devil when things are not going their way when the reality may be that they are fighting against God. Instead of focusing on what you want to do with your life, change your mindset to tell yourself that you can be and do whatever God wants you to be and do.

Seek out God's will for your life, and what He wants you to be. What has God planned and purposed you to be? It is not about what you want. It is about what God wants to do in and through you. You see story after story in history and in Scripture where people thought one thing, but in reality, God was doing something else in their lives.

So, think about where God has positioned you. What has He gifted you to do? What doors has He opened? What doors has He closed? As you talk to Him in that lifestyle of prayer, it becomes clearer what He has planned and purposed for you. Your life is not really all about you. It is all about Him. Even though the Lord has given you so many things to enjoy, the main thing is for you to enjoy Him. Your joy is found in Him. So, as a child, as a pre-teen, as a teen, as a young adult, seek His will, seek His way, dedicate everything about you to Him, and you will see the Lord blow your mind. You will experience Him in ways you never imagined. *Youth Matter*! So go make a mighty impact for the Kingdom of God by putting Jesus on display in everything you do!

Self-Reflection

1. How do you now view this time of your life as a youth?

2. What impacted you the most from this book?

3. What are three things that you will start doing now for your kingdom development and kingdom impact?

Notes

Chapter 1: Introduction

1. Harris, Alex and Brett Harris. *Do Hard Things: A Teenage Rebellion Against Low Expectations*. Multnomah Books: Colorado Springs, 2013.

2. Evans, Tony. *The Kingdom Agenda*. Moody Publishers: Chicago, 2013.

3. See these verses for the indwelling Holy Spirit: John 14:16-17; Romans 8:9; 1 Corinthians 6:19; 1 John 4:4, 13

4. Revelation 21–22

Chapter 2: Your Value

1. Behe, Michael. *Darwin's Black Box: The Biochemical Challenge to Evolution*, The Free Press, New York, 1996. Dembski, William and Jonathan Wells, *How to Be an Intellectually Fulfilled Atheist or Not*, ISI Books: Wilmington, Delaware, 2008. This theory is still being taught in schools even with the lack of evidence for macro-evolution of one kind becoming another kind.

2. This is why the Jesus Christ was born into the world to pay for the sins of mankind. God created humanity in His image and likeness to rule the earth in close relationship to God. Because of our broken relationship with God through our sin, the eternal Son of God, Jesus came into the world to be our representative and perfect sacrifice to pay for our sins. The Lord is actively seeking a relationship with mankind and has shown how serious He is by sacrificing His own Son, Jesus Christ.

3. Smith, Christian. *Soul Searching: The Religious and Spiritual Lives of American Teenagers*. Oxford University Press: Oxford, 2009. See also Dean, Kenda Creasy. *Almost Christian: What the Faith of Our American Teenagers Is Telling the American Church*. Oxford University Press: Oxford, 2010.

4. Here are some of the Old Testament references to the resurrection of the Messiah that the New Testament writers allude to: Psalm 16:10; Psalm 22; Isaiah 53:10-11; Daniel 12:2-3.

Chapter 3: Your Position

1. See Matthew 23:37; Luke 13:34. See also Psalm 68:5; John 1:12; Romans 8:14; 1 Corinthians 8:6; 2 Corinthians 6:18; Ephesians 4:6

2. See also Proverbs 6:20; 23:22

3. If you are in a dangerous or unsafe situation at home contact your local authorities like the police, inform your school, and/or your church so that you may get to safety and get the help you need.

4. Daniel means "God is my judge" was changed to Belteshazzar, which means "Bel protects his life." Hananiah means "Yah(weh) is gracious" was changed to Shadrach which means "the command of Aku" (moon god). Mishael, which means "who is what God is" was changed to Meshach with means "who is like unto Aku" (moon god). and Azariah, which means "Yah(weh) has helped" was changed to Abednego which means "servant of Nebo (Nego)."

5. The dietary laws were an important part of Israel's worship to God. See Proverbs 23:1-3; see also Leviticus 3:17; 11:47; Psalm 141:4; Ezekiel 4:13.

6. See 1 Samuel 16:14-23–26:25

7. Proverbs 21:1

8. Daniel 2:47

Chapter 4: Your Crowd

1. See Genesis 1:27; Genesis 2:18-25

2. Genesis 1:28

3. Galatians 5:22-23

4. See Matthew 4:1-11; Mark 1:12-13; Luke 4:1-13

Chapter 5: Your Development

1. See 1 Samuel 13 & 15

2. 1 Samuel 16:1-13

3. Luke 4:13

Chapter 6: Your Impact

1. See Exodus 6:4-8; Leviticus 18:24-30; Unfortunately, the nation of ancient Israel broke God's covenant by consistent disobedience to God's Word, and in 722 B.C. the Northern Kingdom of Israel was deported by the Assyrians, and then later, in 586 B. C., the Southern Kingdom of Judah was defeated and deported by the Babylonians. This was God's means of discipline to get the nation to follow His Word.

2. 1 Samuel 16

3. 1 Samuel 17:13-14

4. 1 Samuel 10:23

5. Circumcision was a sign of the covenant God gave to Abraham and the nation of Israel. See Genesis 17:10-26; Leviticus 12:3.

6. Daniel 2:47

Chapter 7: Your Growth

1.   2 Peter 1:20-21

2.   The Apostle Peter called the Apostle Paul's writings as Scripture in 2 Peter 3:15-16. Also, the Apostle Paul regarded Luke's writings to be Scripture when he quoted Luke 10:7 along with Deuteronomy 25:4 in 1 Timothy 5:18. The Apostles show an awareness of continuing the ministry of the prophets of old as conveying the Word of God and giving authoritative instruction.

3.   A good resource to start with is Arthur, Kay, David Arthur and Pete De Lacy. *How to Study Youth Bible: Discover the Life-Changing Approach to God's Word*. Harvest House Publishing: Eugene, 2010.

4.   For example, if it is 5th day of the month, read Proverbs chapter 5. If it is the 21st day of the month, read Proverbs chapter 21. If it is the 31st day of the month, read Proverbs chapter 31, and so forth.

5.   Psalm 65:2

6.   See 1 John 5:14-15; also John 14:12-14

7.   Matthew 4:10

8.   Matthew 15:8-9

9.   See John 1:1-3, 12-14, 18

10.   Mark 10:45

11.   See Matthew 20:28; John 13:1-20; Philippians 2:5-8

12.   1 Samuel 12:24

13.   See 2 Corinthians 5:14-15; Galatians 5:13

14.   John 14:15

15.   See John 13:12-16; Philippians 2:3

16.   1 Corinthians 10:24

17.   See Ephesians 4:12; Colossians 1:29

18.   See 1 Corinthians 15:58; Hebrews 6:10

19.   See Romans 12:4-8; 1 Corinthians 12:4-11; 14:1-40; see also Ephesians 4:7-13

20.   1 Peter 4:10-11

21.   Romans 12:3

22. Some believe sharing the gospel is only for those listed in Ephesians 4:11.

23. See also 1 Peter 2:9

24. For further study on spiritual disciplines see Whitney, Donald. *Spiritual Disciplines for the Christian Life*. NavPress: Colorado Springs, 2014 and Evans, Tony. *Life Essentials for Knowing God Better, Experiencing God Deeper, Loving God More*. Moody Publishers: Chicago, 2003.

Chapter 8: Conclusion

1. This story is adapted from Rydelink, Michael. *The Messianic Hope: Is the Hebrew Bible Really Messianic*. B & H Academic: Nashville, 2010, pgs. 185-189.

2. See the introduction of this book.

3. See again Smith, Christian. *Soul Searching: The Religious and Spiritual Lives of American Teenagers*. Oxford University Press: Oxford, 2009, and Dean, Kenda Creasy. *Almost Christian: What the Faith of Our American Teenagers Is Telling the American Church*. Oxford University Press: Oxford, 2010.

About the Author

Daryl Jones is the president and founder of Point Ministries, and also serves as the Lead Pastor of The Rock Fellowship Church in Miami, FL. He excels as pastor, teacher, author, and speaker and his vision is to see a redeemed people of God existing as family living out kingdom values.

Pastor Daryl played wide receiver on the National Championship University of Miami football team of 2001, and went on to play professional football for the New York Giants, Chicago Bears, and the Minnesota Vikings. It was during those years where he began to feel God's pull on his life toward the Gospel ministry.

Pastor Daryl answered the Lord's call to the preach and was licensed and ordained at his home church, New Hope Baptist Church in Dallas, Texas. There, he served as Children's and Youth Pastor. Daryl later served as Youth Pastor at Oak Cliff Bible Fellowship Church in Dallas, Texas, with Dr. Tony Evans, before answering the call to plant The Rock Fellowship Church in Miami, Florida. Pastor Daryl earned a Master of Divinity at Southwestern Baptist Theological Seminary. He is married to Kamica and they have seven wonderful children.

About Point Ministries

Point Ministries is a Christian Bible teaching ministry founded by Pastor Daryl Jones. We exist to glorify God by providing sound Christian biblical teaching through Christian media to make and equip disciples of Jesus Christ to impact the world. We offer sermons, books, prayers, Bible studies, and other teachings to help aid in spiritual growth. Pastor Daryl's sermons can be heard on radio and through internet broadcasts, as well as via various media apps available worldwide. Our goal at Point Ministries is to point you to the Word of God, where Jesus is the Point! Please visit daryljones.org for discipleship resources.

CPSIA information can be obtained
at www.ICGtesting.com
Printed in the USA
LVHW090715201021
700930LV00005B/605